Work and Retirement

Work and Retirement

STANLEY PARKER

London
GEORGE ALLEN & UNWIN
Boston   Sydney

© George Allen & Unwin (Publishers) Ltd, 1982

George Allen & Unwin (Publishers) Ltd,
40 Museum Street, London WC1A 1LU, UK

George Allen & Unwin (Publishers) Ltd,
Park Lane, Hemel Hempstead, Herts HP2 4TE, UK

Allen & Unwin, Inc.,
9 Winchester Terrace, Winchester, Mass. 01890, USA

George Allen & Unwin Australia Pty Ltd,
8 Napier Street, North Sydney, NSW 2060, Australia

First published in 1982

British Library Cataloguing in Publication Data

Parker, Stanley
    Work and retirement.
1. Retirement – Great Britain
I. Title
646.7′9   HQ1064.G7

ISBN 0-04-658238-X
ISBN 0-04-658239-8 Pbk

Library of Congress Cataloging in Publication Data

Parker, Stanley Robert
    Work and retirement
Bibliography: p.
1. Retirement – Great Britain. 2. Aged – Employment – Great Britain. I. Title
HQ1064.G7P37   306′.38′0941   82-4090
ISBN 0-04-658238-X   AACR2
ISBN 0-04-658239-8 (pbk.)

Set in 11 on 12 point Ehrhardt by Fotographics (Bedford) Ltd,
and printed in Great Britain
by Richard Clay (The Chaucer Press) Ltd, Bungay

Contents

Introduction   *page* 11

1   A New Achievement and a Problem   16
    The history of retirement in Britain and the USA; old age and
    retirement in Britain and the USA today; old age and retirement
    in other societies; conclusion

2   The Study of Retirement: Conceptual and Descriptive   31
    Definitions and concepts of retirement; types of retirement;
    types of retired people; attitudes to retirement; case studies; the
    disengagement theory; the activity theory; other theories;
    conclusion

3   Preparation for Retirement   64
    Preference for continued working or retirement; the prospect
    of retirement; influences on attitudes; types of preparation;
    conclusion

4   The Capacity of Older People to Work   81
    Physical changes and capacities; psychological changes and
    capacities; productivity in different kinds of work; employment
    in relation to capacities; conclusion

5   The Experience of Retirement   89
    Reasons for retiring early; reasons for retiring at or after
    pension age; adjustment to retirement; gains and losses; the
    meaning of retirement; health; morale and identity; mortality;
    wives' attitudes to husbands' retirement; conclusion

6   Work after Retirement Age   123
    Employment of older workers; non-employment work; reasons
    for working; demand for work; difficulties and consequences;
    conclusion

7   Retirement as Leisure?   138
    Concepts of retirement and leisure; work/leisure relationships,
    retirement preparation and experience; positive and negative
    views; leisure activities in retirement; new attitudes to leisure;
    conclusion

8   Policy Alternatives   150
    Compulsory or voluntary retirement?; flexible retirement;
    gradual retirement; flexible lifestyles; provision of work; the
    role of education; policies for leisure; the future of retirement;
    conclusion

Bibliography   180
Index   197

To my father, Robert George Parker, one of the many people who enjoy work, have no wish to retire, and are often forgotten when they are forced to do so

Work and Retirement

Introduction

This book is about retirement — the courses of action open to those men and women who have some choice about when and under what conditions they retire, the circumstances in which others have no such choice, and the problems and opportunities of both groups. It is also about work in relation to retirement — the needs which some older but reasonably fit people have for work of some kind and the opportunities which society provides, or increasingly fails to provide, for such work.

Retirement and the work of older people is a very large subject and I am not going to tackle all aspects of it in this book. As a sociologist, I shall concentrate on what work means to older people, their hopes and fears for, and experiences in, retirement, the existing policies of employers, the state and other bodies concerning work and retirement, and in what ways these may be thought to be in need of change. Two topics I shall not attempt to deal with are the complex details of pension scheme legislation and provisions and the question of retirement migration, which has received considerable research attention in France but less in Britain.

The numbers of old people in Britain, along with most other industrial societies, are growing. Between 1961 and 1976 the numbers of people of pensionable age (65 for men, 60 for women) rose by 1·8 million to 9·4 million and are expected to go on rising at least until 1991 (OPCS, 1978). Meanwhile, there are fewer people of pensionable age in some kind of paid employment. In 1931 more than half of the men over 65 were working; in 1951, 31 per cent; in 1971, 19 per cent; and in 1980, 12 per cent (only 10 per cent of women). Over the next few years the figures will almost certainly continue to go down even further.

The ways in which older workers are treated, the frequency of retirement and the particular forms that it takes are not random occurrences — they are the result of deliberate policies formulated and carried out by people with the political, economic or other persuasive power to do so. I shall seek to demonstrate that there are links between a number of causes and effects of work and retirement policies, that certain types of concept, theory, attitude and practice tend not only to reinforce each other but also to represent different broad philosophies or approaches to the whole subject.

11

On the one hand, is an approach to the problems of older people which looks at work and retirement questions from a restrictive, conformist and conservative point of view. Options are preferred, interpretations formulated and facts chosen for emphasis which favour narrowing the range of choice in problematic situations, conforming to existing patterns of thought and behaviour, and generally conserving what has been brought into being. On the other hand, is an approach which takes an expansive, creative and radical point of view. The options, interpretations and choice of facts for emphasis favour widening the range of choice, developing new patterns of thought and behaviour, and generally challenging the *status quo* with alternative policies.

In the first chapter I look at retirement in historical and cultural contexts, noting that it is a comparatively recent development in human society and is a marked feature of only some contemporary societies. The history of retirement in Britain shows first a period of *rare* retirement, when neither the development of the economy nor ideas about the alleged inefficiency of older workers had reached the point at which retirement could be granted to, or imposed upon, the older population generally. This was followed by a period of *discouraged* retirement, when many workers of prime age were in the armed services during the last war and the labour of older workers was needed to replace them. From about the mid-1960s until the present, and likely to continue for some time to come, is a period of *encouraged* retirement as the problem now is not to find workers but to find jobs. Retirement policies have thus been based more on the needs of the economy than on the needs of the people. During the periods of rare and discouraged retirement there were, no doubt, many men and women who would have preferred to retire if they could have afforded to do so. In the present climate of encouraged retirement there are many men and women who would prefer not to retire but are forced to do so.

The second chapter deals with theoretical approaches to retirement. Understanding retirement is a complex and inter-disciplinary matter because the transition from work to retirement involves interactive processes at a number of levels – biological, psychological, social and cultural. But retirement is also something that affects individuals in different ways, as they have

12

varying attitudes to it and varying resources to cope with it – hence we look at a few case studies to put flesh on the bones of theory. Disengagement theory argues that, with increasing age, ties are inevitably severed between an individual and others in his society. The main rival theory – activity – asserts that successful and contented ageing depends on the older individual's continued integration in society, and there is considerable research evidence supporting this assertion. Although some older people do prefer to disengage from society, the theory implying that this is the universal and inevitable pattern is consistent with policies which restrict the opportunities for human development and spontaneity, whereas the activity theory is politically progressive and radical.

Chapter 3 is concerned with the ways in which older workers may prepare for retirement. It is a dream to some, but a nightmare to others. Several sets of people or agencies can play a part in retirement preparation. Educational opportunities open up wider horizons for older people. Some – but not enough – employers offer pre-retirement courses designed to smooth the transition period. Various public and charitable agencies provide information, advice or help in a mostly responsive way, although it is argued that more and better services should be provided. Above all, individuals themselves can prepare and plan for retirement, although it is clear that many at present do not. General approaches to retirement preparation may be summed up as either instructive (telling people what is supposed to be good for them) or participative (encouraging them to work it out in small groups for themselves) – characterised respectively by the top table and round table.

In Chapter 4 we review what is known about the physical and psychological capacities of older people for work, the productivity and general satisfactoriness of older workers, and the relevant implications for employment policies. Although continued employment after late middle age is undesirable in occupations imposing physical strains, this is not the case for most occupations. But stereotypes of older workers and prejudices about them are common and have to be overcome. Theory A – a logical derivation from disengagement theory and the basis for many current retirement practices – posits creeping and irreversible decline in physical and intellectual capacity. Theory

B, while not denying that some changes with age affect some types of employment adversely, emphasises that much of the reduction in working capacity is not inevitable – a position clearly consistent with activity theory.

Chapter 5 is concerned with different aspects of the experience of retirement, including reasons for it, adjustment to it, effects on health and morale, identity and mortality, and wives' attitudes to their husbands' retirement. Unlike the other chapters, this one does not deal primarily with controversial theories, policies or approaches, though on some issues – notably the effect of retirement on health – the evidence is conflicting. The main aim in this chapter is to give an account of the varying experiences of retirement that people have in contemporary Britain and the USA.

Work after retirement age is the subject of Chapter 6. There are several ways in which some form of work features in the lives of people who have passed normal retirement age. The conventional approach is to think in terms of continued employment, either with the same employer or a new one, sometimes with lighter tasks, a change of type of work, or shorter hours. A more creative approach is not against employment for the elderly, but recognises its limitations in meeting their needs for useful activity and so also advocates such non-employment work activities as collective barter of work products or services, or voluntary contributions to educational, welfare or community activities. Not all of the retired population want work (even in the wide sense) but those who do should not be forced to rely on a market economy to provide them with work opportunities. Adequate pensions should provide a financial basis for more elderly people to take part in voluntary and community work, rather than having to rely on the present minimal opportunities for paid employment.

Retirement is often equated with 'leisure' and so in Chapter 7 we examine the similarities and differences between the concepts of retirement and leisure. Research suggests that the ageing process does not normally bring about a fundamental change in leisure behaviour. Patterns of work/leisure relationship have a significant influence on adjustment to retirement. The opposition pattern (work being seen as the opposite of leisure) and the neutrality pattern (the spheres simply being separate) both tend to be restrictive in their consequences for retirement. The extension pattern (work and leisure interpenetrating) offers a better prospect of integrating work and leisure when employment ceases, but preparation for retirement is still important in helping to smooth the transition from work centrality to leisure centrality.

The final chapter is concerned with how we can influence the extent, experience and consequences of retirement in the future. A number of specific but related issues are examined, notably the nature of the retirement decision, the timing and degree of retirement, and preferred lifestyles. The restrictive, conformist and conservative options are compulsory, complete and fixed-age retirement, and linear lifestyles; the expansive, creative and radical options are voluntary, gradual and flexible retirement, and flexible lifestyles. The provision of work for those who need it, the lifelong role of education and positive policies for leisure are all part of a desirable approach to the problems of the elderly. A better future for retirement depends on offering various satisfying roles for older people in our society and on ensuring that informed individual choice is catered for as far as possible.

In this book I examine a large amount of evidence about the realities and possibilities of work and retirement. I take a stand on a number of controversial issues and I seek to show that the general approach or philosophy that I favour – that of being expansive, creative and radical – links the preferred options, interpretations and choice of facts for emphasis. But the commitment is not to 'all' or 'none' – rather it is to 'more' or 'less'. The rival approaches, as exemplified by some of the major issues dealt with in this book, may be summarised thus:

		Approach	
		restrictive/conformist/ conservative	expansive/creative/ radical
Chapter	Topic		
1	Retirement policy based on	'needs' of the economy	needs of people
2	Theory of retirement	disengagement	activity
3	Retirement preparation	'top table', instructive	'round table', participative
4	Stress on	age decrements	combating ageism
6	Key activity concept	employment	work
7	Relation of work and leisure	separation	integration
8	Timing of retirement	fixed-age	flexible
8	Retirement decision	compulsory	voluntary
8	Degree of retirement	complete	gradual
8	Preferred lifestyle	linear	flexible

15

1

A New Achievement and a Problem

The spread of retirement in modern industrial societies has brought both achievements and problems. The institution of retirement is a comparatively recent development in human society and is a marked feature of only some contemporary societies. We examine first the short history of retirement in Britain and the USA, and go on to review the various achievements and problems which retirement has brought to those countries. To set our contemporary situation and attitudes in historical and cultural context, we then look at the ways in which older and retired people are treated in countries outside Britain and the USA.

The History of Retirement in Britain and the USA

A fixed age of retirement is a comparatively modern notion. It was unknown in Britain or elsewhere until the early years of the nineteenth century. Before then, however, there were some precursors of pensionable retirement. The developments, according to Titmuss (1968), took place in three phases during the seventeenth and eighteenth centuries. First, there was sale of an office by the holder to a personally nominated successor. Then a public authority granted a pension to an office holder and charged the cost of this to his successor. Later, a superannuation fund was set up and an Act of 1810 introduced the first non-contributory pension scheme for civil servants. The Northcote–Trevelyan Report had recommended fixed-age retirement on pension as a means of increasing the efficiency of the service by removing those thought to be too old for effective work. An

16

alternative proposal to enable civil servants to retire at whatever age they were judged medically to be incapable of regular, efficient work was rejected as being administratively cumbersome and possibly invidious (Thane, 1978).

Towards the end of the nineteenth century, a fixed retirement age on pension spread to other occupations in the public service and in some large firms. In 1892 elementary schoolteachers received pensions at 60, following acceptance of the argument that low salaries forced many of them to work long past the age at which they ceased to be efficient. In 1890 policemen were awarded pensions after twenty-five years' service, an early retirement age thought suitable to the rigours of the job. By 1896 most non-manual public employees were being pensioned off at 65. Increasing numbers of large firms, such as railway companies, were also retiring their salaried, and sometimes manual, employees on pension. As Thane remarks, the choice of 65 (occasionally 60) as a suitable age for retirement seems to have reflected a popular belief that most people became unfit for regular efficient work at some point in their early 60s. This belief had some foundation in fact, since evidence available to institutions providing the pensions suggested that this was the age at which retirement most frequently became desirable on medical grounds.

From the 1880s there was growing pressure from philanthropic institutions and the trade union movement for state pensions at 65. However, when a means-tested, non-contributory pension was introduced in 1908 it was payable on retirement at 70, in order to save cost to the Treasury. Before state pensions were introduced many old people had to work for as long as they could. For those physically unable to work, pensions brought some financial relief. But for others who were fit enough to work, compulsory retirement brought an abrupt transition from independence to dependency, which they had not chosen and for which they were often unready. It is a harsh judgement, but one with some truth, that there was no retirement problem before the First World War because so few survived their working life (Vickery, 1969).

Although some of the pressure for fixed-age and pensionable retirement came from an awareness that a society richer than ever before should improve its provision for the aged poor, the

17

crucial explanation lay in the growing demands for greater labour efficiency and increased productivity. In the face of foreign competition towards the end of the nineteenth century, the labour process was intensified to increase productivity in a number of occupations such as mining, textiles and engineering. Trade unionists complained that this led to the earlier redundancy of men too old to work at the required pace. Employers both introduced occupational pensions and pressed for a state scheme to allow them to lay off older workers with a clear conscience.

The introduction of the state pension at 70 was immediately followed by demands for its reduction to 65. When mass unemployment in the 1920s led to a demand for lowering the pensionable age in order to release jobs for the younger unemployed, the government brought in a contributory pension for insured workers and their wives for the 65 to 70 age group. The only important change in the state pension scheme up to the present time was the reduction of the female pensionable age to 60 in 1940, following evidence that a much larger minority of women than of men had retired by the age of 60.

After the slump and consequent high unemployment in the early 1930s, the years up to the Second World War saw a gradual revival and development of industry and commerce and thus more employment opportunities. The war itself removed many men of prime age from the labour force and brought about a radically changed attitude to retirement. In 1942, after almost a century of movement towards a fixed retirement age, the Beveridge Report put a forward a view which it would be nice to think reflected a concern with human needs and satisfaction but which, in reality, owed more to the economic exigencies of the time: 'The capacity to work late in life varies from individual to individual. There is no reason to doubt the power of large numbers of people to go on working with advantage to the community and happiness to themselves after reaching the minimum pensionable age.' Subsequently, an incentive to remain at work was offered in the form of a slightly higher state pension for late retirement, although the benefit of this was counteracted by the imposition of an earnings rule limit on pensions operating until five years after minimum pension age.

A New Achievement and a Problem

In the postwar years of full or near-full employment, and indeed shortage of labour in many industries, the emphasis continued to be on encouraging as many old people as possible to remain in, or return to, the labour force. Compared with the prewar period, this represents a change, as Phillipson (1978) puts it, from 'old age as enfeeblement' to 'the elderly as producers'. From the mid-1960s onward we have entered a third phase of the emergence of retirement, and especially of early retirement, since the problem now is not to find workers but to find jobs. It is difficult to escape the conclusion that in all these successive periods of rare retirement, discouraged retirement and encouraged retirement, the elderly have been thought of primarily as a reserve labour force. In the latter period, however, part of the encouragement to retirement is to present it as a social and political right to be guaranteed independently of shifts in the economic climate.

In class and occupational terms, retirement in Britain has undergone a change of image since its inception little more than a century ago. The early superannuated men were those who had been in secure and fairly well-paid jobs – they were middle-class, comfortable and respected. By contrast, when working-class men reached state pension age they were not generally described as retired but as 'old age pensioners', since they usually had no occupational pension and little or no savings. Today the description 'retired' tends to be associated with ex-employees at all levels, though the term 'old age pensioners' is still quite often heard in reference to the poorer sections of the retired population.

A century or more ago retirement simply meant giving up work. With the introduction of pensions a second condition was added: that of financial entitlement. The first condition, however, is the crucial one: retirement as disengagement from work. The retiree is an unemployed person but one on a special register, in that he is openly discriminated against should he wish to return to work (Belbin, 1973). Retirement is thus, in its present form, not something that has been fashioned by human aspirations. It is closely associated with the growth of bureaucracy, government organisations and large companies which have their own reasons for 'retiring' older employees.

19

The history of retirement in the USA is somewhat similar to that in Britain. Forced retirement at a fixed age was very rare in early America, and first appeared for public offices in the late eighteenth century (Fischer, 1977). The idea that a person automatically stopped working at a prescribed age is absent from pre-Civil War definitions of the word 'retirement' (Achenbaum, 1978). Men and women of all ages, not just the elderly, retired under different sets of circumstances. But with the rise of the big business corporation in the early part of the twentieth century there developed an increased interest in rationalising and institutionalising retirement policies. It was argued that the presence of old people in the workforce hampered efficiency. New bureaucratic principles were applied in a deliberate effort to eliminate those who, from a rational point of view, appeared to be inefficient human machines (Achenbaum, 1974).

Old Age and Retirement in Britain and the USA Today

The development of the institution of retirement, and the changes in the lives of individuals and in the norms and values of the societies in which they live, constitute both a set of achievements and a set of problems. In reviewing these achievements and problems, it does seem that the former are outweighed by the latter. The achievements, however, must not be underrated and are considered first. The lists of both achievements and problems are in no particular order, except that more concrete and objective matters are noted first, and more immaterial and subjective matters follow:

(1) *More people are living to a healthy old age in retirement.* As compared with a generation or a century ago, those men and women who survive until pension age may expect to live longer and to do so more healthily, whether in retirement or continuing to do work of some kind. A higher general standard of living (see below) and better health and welfare services are chiefly responsible for this trend.

(2) *There is now a better standard of living for the retired, absolutely if not in comparison with other sections of the*

20

population. The state retirement pension in Britain, although relatively lower than in some West European countries, is fixed at a rate which is intended to take account of inflation of prices, if not of earnings, and the retired population have, at least to some extent, shared in the higher standard of living that has been achieved in the last two decades or so. A recent survey showed that, in addition to the state pension, 84 per cent of those aged 65 or over had a secondary source of income, mostly interest from investments or supplementary benefit (Abrams, 1980). However, only a little over half of the elderly felt that their present sources of income gave them security for the future.

(3)   *The average age of retirement has come down and it is more often voluntary.* Before the Second World War people generally retired only if they were forced to do so by ill-health or if they had substantial other means. Today increasing numbers of employees are retiring before state pension age and are living on occupational pensions. Retirement from a full-time type of work done for most of a person's working life is also followed in some cases by less demanding part-time work as part of a preferred pattern of gradual retirement.

(4)   *The retired population is getting younger, not only in age but also in lifestyle and outlook.* There is a noticeable trend among older people towards more youthful behaviour and a younger outlook. This change − not specifically concerned with retirement norms and values but no doubt connected with them − is probably the result of a combination of the more objective changes noted above. Literature encouraging the elderly to stand up for their rights − such as Alex Comfort's *A Good Age* (1976) − is no doubt also playing a part in this process.

It is difficult to extend the list of achievements relating to retirement much beyond the above, although each of them could no doubt be developed in greater detail. The number of resulting problems, dilemmas and conflicts does, however, seem to be greater:

21

(1) *Demographic pressures are tending to raise the age of retirement, while economic pressures are tending to lower it.* There is a conflict between the growing proportion of elderly to total population (which suggests the desirability of gradually raising the conventional age of retirement) and the increasing scarcity of employment opportunities (which is tending to exert pressure towards earlier retirement). At present, the economic forces seem to be winning: retirement ages – although not state pension ages – are coming down and the adverse effects of a growing proportion of dependent to total population have been masked by the increase in productivity per employee resulting, in the main, from technological innovation. There is a desire, however, among some sections of the retired population for a return to work of some kind, while the trade union movement, being primarily concerned with the interests of its members of normal working rather than retirement age, is generally in favour of earlier retirement.

(2) *There are conflicts between the interests of the retired and the working population.* If the retired are a small proportion of the total population, it is not unreasonable to expect those in employment to be willing to contribute, via taxes, to the cost of providing state pensions. But, as the retired grow in numbers, there may be an increasing reluctance to accept a large 'leisure' class of retirees (Abrams, 1979). A partial answer would be to make occupational pensions universal, but at present only about half of those who retire do so on an occupational pension (Parker, 1980). Also, as competition for jobs grows, older people who stay on in their jobs or who take other employment after retiring from their jobs will increasingly, if unjustifiably, be seen as taking away work from younger people who need it more.

(3) *We tend to relegate the old to non-functional roles.* Once people retire they lose the status and identity they had when they were working. They tend to become 'non-people' in their own eyes and in the eyes of others (Wright, 1975). The leisure of retirement may be pleasur-

22

ably anticipated by those still in employment, but a life of leisure is not a socially recognised virtue in our contemporary society. Prevailing attitudes often result in relegating retired people to stereotypes and pre-established non-functional roles. They are too often left alone to live out a presumed dotage. They are excluded from many communication networks when they lose a place to work. Our society encourages and forces the elderly to become non-problem-solving persons, although without such stimulation most human beings tend to go into a decline (Whitehead, 1978).

(4) *Sudden retirement has bad effects on some people.* Complete and sudden retirement is almost unknown outside industrial society; in most other types of society, there is either no retirement or a gradual sloughing off of the primary occupation. Although retirement means a sudden change in role and status, the individual's conception of himself does not change so rapidly. In this sense, sudden retirement is unnatural and can be the cause of psychological problems of adjustment and identity.

(5) *We are forcing many healthy older people into a retirement they do not want.* The concept of retirement as a desirable phase in everybody's life can be interpreted as a benevolent rule only if work is seen as unpleasant or merely as a means to an end. If it is more than that, then compulsory retirement is not a benevolent rule but a deprivation imposed on the old and weak by the younger and stronger to get them out of the way. The pessimistic view is to accept that an increasing number of elderly men and women, in comparatively good health for their age, will have to resign themselves to living for a good many years in a retirement to which they are psychologically quite unsuited. A more radical view, which we shall consider in detail in the last chapter, is that something can, and should be, done about this situation.

(6) *There are increasing difficulties in satisfying the needs of those older people who prefer work to retirement.* The achievement of better health among the elderly has brought a particular problem of satisfying their need for activity,

23

which in many cases means work of some kind. Older people seeking work – even part-time work – face employers who find it expedient to have fixed-age retirement policies, and trade unions who fear, with much justification, that older workers will be used as cheap labour. Government policies which result in the loss of jobs exacerbate the problem. Furthermore, no real attempt has been made to provide specialist advisory and placing services for older workers, although this has been done in other countries, such as the USA (Showler, 1977).

(7) *There is a lot of unfounded prejudice against the old, particularly relating to their ability to work satisfactorily.* As we shall see in Chapter 4, research on the capacity of older people to work does not support the view that they should be written off as useful contributors. What we are up against is one aspect of ageism: the systematic stereotyping of, and discrimination against, people simply because they are old, just as racism and sexism accomplish this with skin colour and gender. The assumptions for which there is little or no evidence include: the 'right' age for retirement is 65 (or 60, or any particular age); retirement income can be reduced because older people need less money to live on; and it is 'fair' that older people should withdraw from the labour market to make room for younger workers (Withers, 1974). These and similar assumptions reflect prevailing attitudes and institutions but are decidedly not in the interests of older people themselves.

(8) *Age has a low status in our society; we tend to devalue the past.* These two beliefs are related and they combine to make life more difficult and less satisfying for many old people than it need be. To the extent that our contemporary philosophy devalues the past, our society disregards or places a low priority on the needs of the old who are, after all, representatives of the past. The elderly – and particularly the retired elderly – are viewed in invidious stereotypes and are excluded from social opportunities; they lose roles and are given no clear replacement roles,

24

and they often have to struggle to preserve self-esteem through youthful self-images (Rosow, 1974).

(9) *Retirement is seen as the end of life – it needs a new image.* Part of the stereotyping of the period of retirement is that people are expected to conform to society's expectations about it: the retiree is supposed to rest, to mow the lawn occasionally, to visit a little and generally to potter around (Breen, 1963). While this may be an acceptable pattern of life for some, to others it means the end of real life. Society has offered such people few satisfactions apart from work, and when this is taken away many of them can think of little else to live for (Beveridge, 1965). We do not yet accord to retirement and leisure the positive value that we accord to work. We tend to look on retirement as a bench-mark signifying declining physical and mental prowess and impending death.

(10) *We have not yet evolved acceptable norms for retired people.* Because of the relatively recent development of retirement as a near-universal phase of life in our society, and because of the changing composition of the retired population in terms of age, health and general outlook, norms are still evolving for the position of 'retired person'. This creates difficulties for older people, both in the way they see themselves and in the ability of others to respond to them (Atchley, 1972). The retired person is not always sure what he should expect of himself, and other people may feel uncomfortable because they are not sure how to behave towards him. One of the main tasks during retirement is for the individual to discover meaningful ways of relating to society which, in turn, should provide him with an acceptable social identity.

Old Age and Retirement in Other Societies

Retirement is not unknown outside modern industrial societies, but the form it takes and its relationship with the general treatment and roles of the elderly afford some interesting comparisons. After considering some general propositions about the nature of retirement in industrial and agricultural societies, we may take note of the different situations and approaches in various parts of the world.

Up-to-date and fully comparative data about the international incidence of retirement are not easy to find. The general picture, as of the 1950s, was that among males aged 65 and over, only 38 per cent were working in industrialised countries, 61 per cent in semi-industrialised societies and 70 per cent in predominantly agricultural countries (Riley and Foner, 1968). In other words, with increasing industrialisation and a higher standard of material living, the proportion of older men needed to contribute to the wealth of their society, and hence having the opportunity to do so, declines. To generalise about the three patterns relevant to varying degrees of industrialisation: stable agricultural countries retain a high percentage of their elderly in employment because work is mainly on the land and is a way of life; agricultural countries on the road to industrialisation (and consequently in a state of economic flux) have older workers who are excluded from the new types of work, while having lost the economic security deriving from land ownership or tenure; while advanced industrial countries show the 'institutionalised' pattern of retirement that we have already considered.

There are several differences between rural and urban life, or between 'simpler' and industrialised societies, which influence both the incidence of retirement and the forms it takes. First, there is less age-grading in rural societies, chiefly because it is less pertinent to the main occupational roles. Secondly, there is more self-employment in rural societies, which means that the individual is more able to control whether he works or not and when he may give up work. Thirdly, because of the need to keep down the proportion of the dependent to working population, there is less tolerance of the non-work role. Fourthly, retirement is frequently associated with the transfer of property to children or younger relatives. Fifthly, a higher proportion of women also work, and so they share in the arrangements for retirement. Sixthly, more is expected to be done by children for their aged and retired parents, with whom living quarters are often shared (Bauder and Doerflinger, 1967).

Although there is usually no formal retirement in pre-literate

26

and simpler societies, the old men are not expected to keep on being hunters or warriors or farmers. They are commonly promoted to become elders, headmen or priests. In other words, they shift from roles requiring much physical exertion to sedentary, advisory or supervisory positions. Cessation of work in most pre-literate societies occurs only when the individual, regardless of age, has lost his physical or mental ability to engage in socially useful activities, or is so defined by his culture (Clark, 1972).

Respect for, and high status accorded to, the aged in simpler societies stems from their role as transmitters of culture and from the greater importance attached to tradition and continuity rather than to novelty and change. However, the role of the aged, and the consequent general attitudes to them, vary between different types of simpler society. The evidence indicates that when conditions called for respect to the aged they got it; when these conditions changed they might lose it (Simmons, 1945). But respect for aged men has offered no assurance of the same status for women. If either sex has lost respect in old age, it has been more likely to be the women than the men.

Turning now to the more contemporary world, we may note some differences in the ways in which older people are treated and how the question of retirement is dealt with. In Eastern Europe generally, where rural traditions persist despite some industrialisation, age is not necessarily associated with decline nor is it considered, in itself, to be a valid reason for retirement (Zborowski and Herzog, 1952). In the Soviet Union, doubling the average pension and including members of collective farms in the formal pension system in the mid-1960s have tended to promote withdrawal from the labour force. At the same time, the Soviet government has taken measures to encourage older people to work; for example, they can work and still receive 50–100 per cent of their pension (Rowland, 1975).

A rather similar situation pertains among the Hutterite community in the USA. There is no arbitrary age of retirement for these people. If, for example, an elderly man is removed from a supervisory position he is often simultaneously elected to a position on the council. No elderly person is forced to choose between the extremes of doing nothing or holding a full-time job

(Hostetler, 1974). The collective settlements in Israel follow a somewhat similar pattern. Retirement from work is gradual and does not entail an abrupt and complete break from work routines and responsibilities. Ageing members are not suddenly relieved of their major social function. Inevitably, as they lose their capacity for hard physical work, they gradually become part-time workers and are eventually transferred to lighter tasks (Talmon, 1961).

In the traditional Confucian family of China, once men and women became grandparents they could choose whether or not they wished to continue to manage households (in the case of women), or to operate family businesses or property or hold public office (in the case of men). Retirement did not mean loss of authority in decision-making: they were always consulted and had the final word in family councils. Withdrawal from some activities did not mean complete loss of other functions, such as scholarly pursuits and religious duties (Blitsten, 1963). To some extent these arrangements continue in modern China. The government programme stipulates that men can retire from the age of 55, women from 50. How completely an individual actually retires depends on his needs and health, and the needs of his community. The Chinese retiree plays an important role as a transmitter of skills and cultural heritage, although it must be remembered that about 80 per cent of older workers earn their living from the land (Liu, 1974).

In Japan well over half of the aged men continue to work – a much higher proportion than in the USA or Britain. The feeling in Japan, especially among the aged, is that every able person should work as much and as long as possible. Those who continue to work are generally more respected than those who do not. The customary 'retirement age' in most businesses is about 55, but 'retirement' usually means simply switching to another company, another job in the same company, or to self-employment. More than half of Japanese workers aged 55 or over are farmers, lumbermen, or fishermen (Palmore, 1975).

In other parts of the world, too, retirement is either rare or gradual but hardly ever complete at a fixed age. Retirement is unknown among the peasants of the Andes (Holmberg, 1961) and the Abkhasia people of the Caucasus mountains (R. Jones,

28

1977). Healthy people continue to work, although in reduced form, just as long as they are physically able to do so. In the backward but industrialising republic of Panama, in 1972, less than two out of every five workers were covered by public old age pensions, so few workers could afford to retire (Jaffe and Rios, 1975). By contrast, in the more stable and traditional Burmese society both older men and women retire from economic activity and are expected to devote themselves to religious duties, including the performance of good deeds and meditation (Rustom, 1961).

Finally, it would be wrong to imagine that retirement is unknown among all tribal societies and that old age is always accorded respect. Among the Nyakyusa of the Great Basin of Africa 'retirement' is said generally to begin at about 35, though this usually means not clinging to certain positions which are made available to the next generation (Koller, 1968). The aged among the Baganda in East Africa have no tradition of societal leadership, but only of advice, storytelling and trying to be good grandparents – in fact, not unlike the role of the elderly in Western societies (Nahemow and Adams, 1974). With the spread of education the position of the aged as advisors is weakened, and their role as repositories of the oral traditions and wisdom of the past is less valued.

Conclusion

In Britain and the USA retirement was virtually unknown until the early nineteenth century. It started to grow in the years before the Second World War, but the consequent shortage of labour during and just after the war period meant that older workers were encouraged to remain in, or re-enter, the labour force. Fixed-age retirement and occupational pensions developed alongside bureaucracies and large companies and were spurred on by the belief that older workers were slowing down overall productivity in increasingly competitive markets. Thus, in short, there were successive periods of rare retirement, discouraged retirement and encouraged retirement. A comparison of the economic situation and the prevailing 'official' attitudes to retirement during these successive periods strongly suggests that retirement practices and attitudes in modern industrial societies owe more to a concern with the 'needs' of the economy than with the needs of individual men and women.

Retirement is rare outside modern industrial societies and in simpler societies there is generally more respect for, and status accorded to, the elderly because they have a more significant role to play in the life of the community. In many parts of the world today retirement is either rare or gradual, but hardly ever complete at a fixed age.

2
The Study of Retirement: Conceptual and Descriptive

As a concept, retirement is deceptively simple. It has an accepted commonsense meaning of 'giving up work', yet this hides a number of implications which need to be spelt out before serious attempts at theory-building can be made. There are different types of retirement, of retired people, and of attitudes to retirement: these types can be delineated conceptually and then illustrated by case studies of how men and women actually face and cope with retirement. Although 'disengagement' and 'activity' are often referred to as theories of *retirement*, they are, more accurately, broader theories of ageing. Nevertheless, these two theories deserve our close attention, as they make an important contribution to the two general approaches to work and retirement which we are considering throughout this book.

Definitions and Concepts of Retirement

Most dictionaries give several different definitions of retirement. Some of these are irrelevant to our concerns in this book, for example, 'retirement' meaning 'going to bed'. Other definitions, while not exactly describing the phenomena we are interested in, nevertheless give a flavour of it. Thus drawing back, retreating, receding, withdrawing from society, public or active life, or occupation are all associated with the process, event and condition we are dealing with.

Some writers prefer a single definition of retirement, often selecting their own definition from a range which they acknowledge. For example, Moore and Streib (1959) define a retired person as 'one who has relinquished his mid-life job or position for a life of greater freedom and leisure and who relies on other sources than wages, salaries or profits for the major portion of his current living'. They believe that this definition is not so strict as to exclude those who engage in some productive effort nor so broad as to include those who have merely shifted to another full-time job. Certainly this definition is preferable, in terms of the range of behaviour and attitudes we are trying to comprehend, to narrow definitions such as those of Hinds (1963) and Kaplan (1979). The former takes retirement to mean 'to withdraw from business, active service or public life', while the latter defines a retiree as 'one who withdraws, temporarily or permanently, from any sphere of activity, interest or commitment'. The concession that retirement can be temporary is in the right direction, but the definition fails to make it clear that retirement can also be partial or complete.

Atchley (1976) is among those writers who insist that receipt of a pension is a necessary feature of retirement. He sees retirement as 'a condition in which an individual is forced or allowed to retire and is employed less than full-time . . . and in which his income is derived at least in part from a retirement pension earned through prior years of service as a job holder'. Although this definition no doubt applies to a large proportion of self-defined retired persons in the USA, it is much less applicable in Britain, where nearly half of the men and seven out of eight of the women who retire before state pension age receive no occupational pension (Parker, 1980). Also definitions such as Atchley's imply that part-time working accompanied by an occupational pension constitutes 'retirement', whereas it seems more likely that people in that position would see themselves as in process of gradual retirement rather than in the condition of retirement: they are likely to say, 'I have retired from my main life work but am still working part-time at something else'.

Other writers recognise the plurality of definitions available and select some of them for special mention. For example, Tibbitts (1954) notes three meanings of retirement: it is 'generally understood to mean separation or withdrawal from one's principal or career occupation in gainful employment', it may 'come to mean complete or final separation from the work force' or it may 'denote the end of all contributory activity

32

beyond that of mere self-maintenance'. Back (1969) distinguishes between economic and social retirement. With the former, a person severs economic relations with an employer and receives a pension, while the latter means conceding that he is no longer active in his life career. Evans (n.d.) offers the prescriptive, but to me the wholly congenial, thought that 'the retired person is an abdicant from his customary occupation, but not from work; he yields to the one, but he should not relinquish the other. In retirement if anything stays let work stay.'

Definitions of retirement may be either objective (criteria laid down by someone else) or subjective (self-defined). Using the definition of retirement as having worked at some time during the last twenty years but not now working or seeking work for pay, a recent British national survey found that the correspondence of objective and subjective definitions varied from 54 per cent of 'retired' women under pension age to 98 per cent of 'retired' men over pension age (Parker, 1980). In the USA Palmore (1965) noted that retirement rates varied widely depending on the measure used. For example, if any person not working full-time all the year is considered retired, this would have applied to 87 per cent of the men and 97 per cent of the women aged 65 or older in 1962. But if only those who had not worked at all during the year are considered to be retired the figures would be 64 per cent and 87 per cent respectively. In an attempt to understand subjectively defined retirement, Irelan and Bell (1972) found that labour-force status was the best single predictor, with receipt of social security benefits the next best.

Perhaps Bixby (1976) best sums up the variety of definitions of retirement and the legitimacy of using different definitions for different purposes: 'No single concept or measure of retirement is accepted, either by social gerontologists or policymakers . . . It may relate to the extent or continuity of work or earnings . . . to the termination of a specific career . . . to receipt of a retirement pension, or to an individual's perception of his status, or to some combination of these factors.' Mitchell (1972) expresses a similar thought that retirement may be a state of mind, a way of life, an economic or social condition or, as is more likely, a complex of them all.

33

Turning briefly to more general conceptual approaches to retirement, we may note that understanding retirement is an interdisciplinary matter because the transition from work to retirement involves interactive processes at a number of levels – biological, psychological, social and cultural (Carp, 1968). It is important to recognise that retirement is a highly complex phenomenon and is interrelated with other social variables and processes; it needs to be studied in its interaction with other institutions in the social system (Kasschau, 1976). It can be demonstrated, for example, that retirement rates are correlated with the state of the local labour market, and that a combination of administrative convenience and what is believed to be true about declining work capacities with age explain much of the variation in employers' policies concerning retirement.

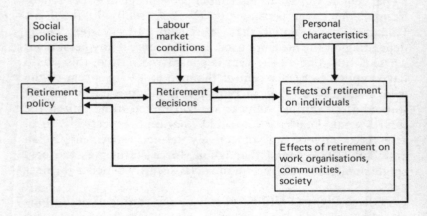

Figure 2.1

A dynamic model of the causes and effects of retirement policies and decisions has been put forward by Atchley (1979) (see Figure 2.1). Retirement policies are initially influenced by general social policies such as public support for older adults or the concept of 'social insurance' and by labour-market conditions such as redundancies, labour shortages and unemployment. The retirement decision concerns whether persons will retire or remain employed and, if they retire, when. Retirement decisions are influenced by retirement policies, labour-market conditions and personal characteristics such as health, employability, availability of income or assets, or desire for retirement. Retirement may involve physical, social, psychological, or financial effects on individuals. In addition, retirement may have effects on the productivity or financial well-being of work organisations, or effects on the economic and political structure of communities. Retirement may also have financial and labour-market impacts on society at large. The results of retirement feed back into retirement policy.

The ingredients of this model, although complex, are more interactive than they are depicted. For example, social policies are themselves influenced by, as well as influencing, other features of society and the same applies to at least the attitude components of personal characteristics. However, models such as this are a useful reminder that to tackle effectively one feature of society and of individual life, such as retirement, means in some degree also to tackle a number of other relevant features.

Types of Retirement

A major subdivision of retirement is whether it occurs before normal retirement or pension age ('early'), at that age ('on time'), or after ('late'). This subdivision, however, is essentially of the timing of retirement rather than of variations in its content or meaning. One of the commonest distinctions made is between voluntary and involuntary retirement, although it is not always easy to see where the one ends and the other begins. If a person responds to an employer's call for volunteers to retire, or if he announces that he is giving up a job that is still open to him, then the act is certainly voluntary. But if he reaches mandatory retirement age in a job and accepts the situation willingly, is it voluntary or compulsory? Or if he is 'forced' into retirement by ill-health rather than by any action of his employer, then which category does this fall into?

35

Assuming, for the sake of further analysis, that it does make some sort of sense to distinguish between voluntary and involuntary retirement, we may examine what difference this makes to the retirement experience itself. One obvious implication is that planning and preparation are more likely to be features of voluntary than of involuntary retirement. Although the knowledge that one is going to have to retire is normally available well in advance, there is less incentive to plan if the retirement is not wanted at that time or at all. Where the timing of the retirement is the responsibility of the employer there is a temptation for the employee to sit back and wait for it to happen. Where retirement is keenly anticipated and the timing set by the employer or the pension scheme is acceptable to the employee, the difference between 'voluntary' and 'involuntary' retirement is negligible. But where retirement is both imposed and unwanted the difference may be appreciable.

A limited amount of research has been concerned with what it feels like to be retired voluntarily and involuntarily. The general picture, not surprisingly, is that voluntary retirement tends to be viewed and experienced more positively than does involuntary retirement. In their study of men living in a retirement hotel in Chicago, Peretti and Wilson (1975) found that many who had retired voluntarily had planned to do so for several years and they had taken various steps to keep occupied and to secure a reasonable income. The involuntarily retired men, however, felt that 'forced' retirement had disrupted their everyday way of life. They had not considered the move, and when it came there was an abrupt change in their lifestyle. For some, the term 'retirement' was negative and carried a stigma.

From their Cornell study, Thompson, Streib and Kosa (1960) analysed retirees into four categories. First, there were the *willing voluntary* ones, those whose pre-retirement attitudes were favourable and who made the decision to retire themselves. A second group were *willing administrative* retirees, with favourable pre-retirement attitudes but who had to retire under company rules. A third group were *reluctant voluntary* retirees, who held unfavourable attitudes but nevertheless chose personally to retire, frequently for health reasons. Finally, there were the *reluctant involuntary* retirees, whose attitudes were unfavourable and for whom company policy made retirement mandatory. According to the writers, 'it would appear that the willing retirees are no more likely to become dissatisfied than are those who remain gainfully employed; but that those who are reluctant to retire are very much more likely to become dissatisfied'.

Belbin and Clark (1970) have devised a typology which owes less to retirement attitudes and more to a combination of timing and degree of flexibility of employers' retirement policies. Groups that show a higher percentage of retired persons than does the general population are called *premature* retirement, examples being the armed forces, miners and single men. Groups that tend to have a lower percentage of retired persons than the general population are *delayed* retirement, including unskilled manual workers, construction workers and married men. Those tending to have a relatively high percentage of retired persons before the normal age, but a lower percentage thereafter, are the *flexible* retirement group, including many employers and managers, and salespeople. Fourthly, those having a lower than average percentage of retired persons before pension age but thereafter a higher percentage are the *rigid* retirement group, such as many skilled manual and engineering workers.

Yet another categorisation of retirement is offered by Havighurst and Shanas (1953) who were concerned with the type of transition made possible. They distinguished five types: arbitrary retirement at a fixed age; the tapering-off of activity in terms of duration; slowing down, such as turning over responsibility to a successor; taking a lower level job in a hierarchy; and taking a different and less demanding position in another work situation. The authors were particularly concerned with professional workers and they concluded that, where such workers are offered a choice, they prefer to slow down or to take a lower level job in another work situation rather than to retire from work completely.

Types of Retired People

Time has an effect on the experience of retirement in two different ways. First, it may mean that people who have only recently retired will have done so under conditions somewhat different from those who retired perhaps two or three decades ago. Secondly, it may be that there are successive phases in most retirements which tend to make the experience different at each phase.

In Britain, Walker (1980) has discerned two types of retired person: the newly retired and the very elderly. Although there is no dividing line between the two groups (which together show a series of gradations rather than a sharp break), it seems a fair generalisation to say that the former group are materially less disadvantaged than the latter. The recently retired have more access to newly emerging resources such as earnings-related state pensions, occupational pensions and savings schemes. By contrast, the homes of the very elderly are more likely to need repair and their stock of consumer durables is likely to be low or to need replacement. A somewhat similar situation is to be found in the USA, where Cain (1967) refers to the more favoured group as the 'new old', in contrast to those who retired in the years after the Second World War. The respective material circumstances of these groups do not, of course, necessarily imply that retirement today is felt to be a happier or more acceptable state than it was in the past.

The second temporal distinction is what happens over time to the same person in retirement. References to 'phases' of retirement are fairly common in the literature, but there is not much agreement about what these are. Moore and Streib (1959) refer to an initial period which may be of elation or regret, followed by a feeling of being depressed, dissatisfied, or 'lost', leading later to satisfaction or contentment. Hinds (1963) also sees a first phase of elation or despondency in the weeks or months after retirement, followed by a period of 'realism and attempted stabilization' during which the individual accepts retirement as irreversible and makes a determined effort to settle down. The third phase envisaged by Hinds is of withdrawal and decline, failing health and strength and the risk of becoming a geriatric problem.

Cesa-Bianchi and his colleagues (1970) link their discussion of phases of retirement to theories of disengagement and activity which we shall consider below. Basing their conclusions on a study of post-retirement patterns in Milan, they believe that for about the first five years after retirement there is generally 'a sense of satisfaction and therefore one can speak of a correspondence between disengagement and satisfaction'. Then, as time passes, people become dissatisfied because of their inability to do many of things they enjoyed in the past. At this point, generally after about the age of 70, they can go one of two ways: they can become more active or they can become accustomed to disengagement.

A simpler division than those considered so far is into early and later retirement. Where there is a change of attitude from the earlier to the later period, it may be expected to be often some kind of swing of the pendulum or regression to an earlier norm. Thus those who resist retirement at first may learn to enjoy their greater free time later. But others who volunteer for, or willingly accept, retirement may, at first, underestimate the force of habit and may later find time hanging heavily on their hands or the loss in status accompanying retirement difficult to bear (Pollak, 1948).

It is clear that most of those who write about phases of retirement recognise that at one or more points in their life after retirement most people have some sort of choice about what to make of it. Perhaps it goes without saying that others have only the one phase – they are lucky enough to find retirement wholly desirable, fulfilling and satisfying, or they are unlucky enough to detest every minute of it. For the rest there are phases, each one in some sense a product of the previous situation or state of mind. It will become clear from research reviewed and case studies presented in the rest of this chapter that ways of coping with retirement and attitudes to it are so varied as to make it overambitious, in the present state of our knowledge or perhaps ever, to delineate phases of retirement which apply to the experience generally.

Howe (1980) complains, with some justification, that much retirement research deals almost exclusively with the male workforce. Certainly, there is no reason to exclude working women from research which deals with the retirement experiences and attitudes of working people. The only justification for questioning the relevance of the concept of retirement to non-employed

39

housewives is that a woman who is, largely or entirely, a housewife seldom retires completely from that role until she leaves home or is dead (Rhee, 1974). In the wider sense of leaving one role or status for another, many women 'retire' several times in their switches between preoccupation with work or family life. It is worth noting, in passing, that women who have retired from work, as compared with lifelong housewives, have no fewer social resources and appear to be more socially involved (Fox, 1977).

As a prelude to our discussion of the theory of disengagement later in this chapter, we may look briefly at types of retired person relevant to these theories. From her studies in San Francisco, Lowenthal (1966) described four types in terms of retirement compulsion and disengagement: first, the involuntarily disengaged (those who were compulsorily retired and who withdrew from social activity); secondly, the voluntarily disengaged (who were not compulsorily retired but withdrew); thirdly, the voluntarily engaged (not compulsorily retired, did not withdraw); and fourthly, the involuntarily engaged (compulsorily retired, did not withdraw). She found that the first type ranked lowest on measures of morale and the third group ranked highest.

Belbin's (1972) relatively simple dichotomy is concerned with two retirement 'archetypes' in terms of activity. The first shows a low level of activity, a routine way of life and adjustment to a specific and restricted environment. The second has a high level of activity, interest in new learning and experiences, and 'well-preserved' abilities. Of someone in the first group Belbin writes he 'may yet count as one of the successfully disengaged'. More positively, people in the second group are said to enjoy 'a high or medium-high satisfaction in retirement'.

Attitudes to Retirement

In this section, instead of using objective criteria such as time, phases, gender, degree of activity or disengagement to distinguish types of retirement, the categories are more in terms of subjective variables such as flexibility and attitudes.

40

The theme of flexibility appears in the analyses of several writers on the subject of retirement. Havighurst (1954) was among the earliest to point out the importance of flexibility in the process of adjusting, or failing to adjust, to retirement. For most people the set of habits which constitute a role is changed only with difficulty. To change roles easily and increase or reduce activity in a given role requires a personal quality which Havighurst calls 'role flexibility'. It seems that an important ingredient for a smooth and successful transition from work to retirement is the ability to shift from the work role to other social roles (Loether, 1975). People who are unable to substitute other social roles for the lost work role often find retirement a traumatic experience, to which they may eventually adjust only by accepting 'disengagement'.

Flexibility during working life does not necessarily mean frequent changes of occupation, but it does imply flexibility in playing the occupational role so that elements in that role may be continued into retirement. It is perhaps useful to make a distinction between three types of working life: a job or succession of jobs very similar to each other; an orderly career or progression of jobs; and a disorderly or chaotic career with jobs bearing little or no relation to each other. The same or similar job holder will be less likely than the others to have developed the flexibility to cope easily with retirement, in the absence of a long and well-thought-out preparation. The individual who has experienced an orderly and progressive career will bring to the retirement status a better capacity to explore alternatives and to see retirement (paradoxically, in view of its literal meaning) as advancement. The person with a disorderly career may also cope reasonably well, retirement being perceived as yet another change in direction (Maddox, 1966). On the face of it, we appear to have two groups out of three with a good prognosis for retirement, but it must be remembered that the first type – with the same job or similar jobs – is the most numerous of the three in our present society.

Writers on the theme of retirement show a remarkable inventiveness in delineating types of attitude to it. Often the types consist of a mixture of objective and subjective elements, status/positional and attitudinal factors. Thus Barrett (1972) discerns four types: those who achieved adequate status as adults and are happy to rest on their laurels; those who have been unable to achieve any position of esteem and have accepted it; those whose need for status is satisfied through their non-work contacts; and unhappy people who are still seeking status. This does seem to be a particularly status-ridden analysis and hardly relevant to those retirees, perhaps few in number in the USA but more numerous elsewhere, who can live quite happily and even 'creatively' without ever thinking about status.

A categorisation which makes no claim to apply to other than professional people is that of Snow and Havighurst (1977). They offer two types: transformers and maintainers-reorganisers. Transformers change their lifestyle by reducing their professional activity by choice and creating for themselves, in retirement, a new and enjoyabe lifestyle. Maintainers-reorganisers hold on to professional activity successfully after 'retirement', generally pursuing part-time assignments. Seventy-seven per cent of transformers were reported to be happy in retirement, but only 50 per cent of maintainers-transformers. Perhaps all work involvement and no leisure activity makes Jack a dull retiree.

In what he describes as 'lay observations', Mitchell (1972) divides retirees into three groups: the average solid citizen type; the preferred retirement risk group; and the problem cases. The first only occasionally think in middle life about retirement, become more concerned with it as time passes, but largely in terms of prospective economic security. The second group 'want nothing so much as to get away from the nine-to-five rat race, to get to that Shangrila in Florida, or to indulge themselves in long-denied pursuits of their own choosing'. Somewhat against the grain of other research findings, Mitchell describes this group as 'generally well-adjusted and will make it on their own'. His third group are the problem cases who consume but do not produce, exist but do not really live.

A more rigorous, but in some ways not dissimilar, typology is put forward by Riesman (1954). His concern is with ageing, in general, rather than with retirement, in particular, and his three types are autonomous, adjusted and anomic. After middle life, some people bear within themselves psychological sources of self-renewal: ageing brings wisdom with no loss of spontaneity and ability to enjoy life, and they are relatively independent of the strictures and penalties imposed on the aged by contemporary culture. Others have no such resources within them but are the beneficiaries of a cultural preservative (derived from work, power, position, and so on) which sustains them at a reasonably adjusted level. A third group, the anomic, protected neither from within nor from without, simply decays.

An analysis of five personality types in relation to adjustment to retirement is offered by Reichard, Livson and Peterson (1968). The first category is of 'mature men' who accept retirement easily, without regrets over the past, and are able to find new tasks and cultivate new relationships to occupy their time. Second, are the 'rocking-chair men' who welcome retirement as a time to sit back, relax and passively enjoy their old age. Then there are the 'armoured men' who develop an active, highly organised lifestyle to defend themselves against the anxieties of growing old. The two remaining categories are said to be poor in their adjustment to retirement: the 'angry men' are unable to face the prospect of growing old, sometimes bitterly blaming others for their failure to achieve their life goals, and the 'self-haters' blame themselves for their misfortunes and often sink into depression. Apart from the fact that it ignores women retirees completely, my main quarrel with this categorisation is that it leaves out those who do not really like retirement but who come to make the best of it – what might be called the 'sad park-bench people'.

Having reviewed many – but by no means all – possible types of personal characteristics and attitudes to retirement, we are left with the difficult task of taking stock of what these propositions and findings actually reveal about the varying experience of retirement. Some of the statements put forward and conclusions drawn seem to tell us more about the values and culture of the researchers and theorists than about how the man or woman in the street feels when he or she approaches and comes to live in retirement. To some extent the credibility and usefulness of the various analyses is a personal preference, and on this basis I would conclude that three of the most important concepts in understanding retirement are phases, flexibility and resources. Phases underline the influence of time and the sequence of actions and reactions following the event of retirement. The degree of flexibility shown by the individual determines how adequately the process of adjustment will be handled. Finally, resources which, if they are present, may be economic or social, internal or external, influence the rate and direction of adjustment, if it takes place at all.

Case Studies

The ways in which retirement affects individuals vary according to their circumstances and attitudes. Sample surveys (such as those quoted above and others which we shall consider in Chapters on the experience of retirement) can tell us much about retirement behaviour and attitudes in the aggregate, but they afford little insight into the deeper meaning of retirement to individual men and women. Also, the judgement about how far disengagement, activity or any other theory is adequate to account for the variety of retirement behaviour and attitudes needs to be made in the light of a set of total human experiences as well as of more quantitative data obtained from sample surveys.

There are as many stories of retirement to be told as there are instances of retirement. In selecting the following case studies I have had in mind those which feature contrasting circumstances, attitudes and modes of coping with retirement and those which illustrate some of the theoretical types discussed above. The four cases do not 'prove' any particular theory of retirement – they simply show the different ways in which four people have faced retirement and have become more or less adjusted to it.

(1) *Norman*
Norman is 62 and retired from a senior management position a year before he would have had to do so under the company's mandatory retirement policy. During the last year or so of his employment he developed a rather undefined sense of dissatisfaction with his work. As a manager, his life was being made

increasingly difficult by union attitudes, and he felt he was not handling staff problems too well. So when the opportunity arose of retiring early he took it. He has a good pension and lives with his wife and son in a very comfortable detached house with a large garden.

Norman had not prepared himself in any way for retirement and had no particular plans to get another job. 'I launched myself quite rapidly into retirement. It shows how life can laugh at you . . . I argued with myself that I had reached a certain point in my career. I was told I wouldn't get promotion. I reasoned that I would be better off if I retired because I wouldn't have the aggro and would be able to do what I wanted to do and not what other people wanted me to do.'

Would Norman consider taking up another job? At the time of his retirement he had several offers but turned them all down. 'I rather like not working. I don't particularly wish to get up every morning and take up cudgels with the rest of the world.' But he is aware of a certain loss of status now that he is retired. 'I had a large office, a secretary, and a work-based status. When I went to the occasional office dinner, I was very conscious that everybody there had a status, a kind of label on their coat. I would now have no label. If I had to explain "I'm a sales manager, retired", people would switch off. Nobody is interested in a retired person's view. You would be attempting to retain a professional status without the profession.'

Norman didn't slide into retirement – he jumped into it. 'To a certain extent it is a leap into the unknown. The only way to find out what it's like is to do it. I didn't want to do it half and half.' His three main activities in retirement are golf, computing and travel. He has developed the first two interests only since retirement, and even travel was nothing more than a vague aspiration before that. He plays golf once or twice a week and finds no shortage of people to play with. He recently bought a small home computer and has attended evening classes in computer technology and programming: 'It's an open-ended challenge from a mental point of view. There is no limit to what you want to do – the limitation is in yourself. The future lies in the use of computers . . . I want at least to understand what is going on.'

During the three years of his retirement Norman has travelled with his wife quite extensively in Europe, the USA and Australia. He has been to places he would not have seen had he kept working. 'If you're 60 you're using up valuable and limited time: the more years you work, the less inclined you are to do anything adventurous in the way of travel. There are certain things which it pays you to do early on, and not to wait until it's too late. Retirement was a leap in the dark but it was supported by my view that there's more in life than work.'

Before retirement Norman was fairly active in his community, doing youth and charity work. In the last two or three years he has tended to reduce that activity. 'People ask me to go on some committee; they say "You can do this now you're retired", and I've tended to react against that. Although I've had one new voluntary job since I've retired, I had much more important jobs earlier. I suppose there is a causative relationship between my attitude to retirement and to voluntary work. In both cases I don't want to get involved in hassling with people.'

Norman believes that people are either inherently happy or nervous of the future, and clearly puts himself in the former category. He sums up his situation in a matter-of-fact way: 'After a very satisfactory career, I reached a point where work was becoming a burden. So I side-stepped the situation and retired. Five years before I retired I was embedded in employment. Being retired is like learning a new language. The basis of life changes, and in my case it has definitely changed for the better.'

(2) Arthur

Arthur, a bachelor, retired five years ago when he was 65. He worked as a messenger and had done so for many years, ever since leaving the army in 1945. He did not want to retire and felt fit enough to carry on working, but his employer said he had to go. He has a very small occupational pension (not index-linked) in addition to his state pension, and lives in a small council flat. His income is only just enough to maintain a modest standard of living, with few luxuries.

'I think they treat the old folk very shabbily. Until they told me I had reached the age when I had to retire I had worked all my years in a useful occupation. Then they threw me on the scrap heap. I looked around for another job but there just weren't any to be had. I'd always been used to going out every day and not having a job to go to hit me very hard. For a time I used to go and see my old mates once or twice a week just for a chat, but then it dropped off. At the beginning I thought I might get another job because I knew a few people round the city, but gradually it dawned on me that I'd had it.'

Arthur had few hobbies or non-work interests when he was employed, and retirement faced him with empty days that he had somehow to fill. 'I still get up at the same time every morning even though I know I don't have to. For a time I used my free bus pass to take a ride into town and walk around the parks in summer or the museums in winter, but I got fed up doing that after a time and don't do it much now. I didn't know what to do with my time when I retired – and I still don't know.'

One of Arthur's few interests is reading library books, especially on historical and transport subjects. He was encouraged by an acquaintance – he doesn't feel he has any friends – to visit his local day centre for the elderly, but it didn't seem to be a very happy experience for him. 'The trouble is you can't hold an intelligent conversation with the lot that get there. All they want to do is natter and drink cups of tea. I reckon I've got something better to do with my time than fritter it away there.'

Arthur is not yet a recluse, but is going in that direction. His resentment at being retired is still strong and he clearly rejects the role of 'retired person' that he feels has been thrust on him. 'Most of the population despise old people, and I must admit there are times when I despise myself. I know I'm lucky to have good health for someone of my age, but what's the good of health if you can't lead a useful life? I'm not one of those who can just sit in a chair all day and do nothing, and I don't want all the silly games they expect you to play. Leisure? I've never known what leisure is. I don't see why people like me can't have a little job and earn a few bob. It's a lousy system that takes people's jobs away from them, and I don't believe that there isn't the work to be done if things were organised properly . . . '

(3) *Meg*
Meg is a retired professional civil servant aged 61 who last

worked full-time three years ago. Having worked for thirty years in the same department, she had reached a senior and well-paid position, and for the last twelve months of her employment she chose to work part-time hours. She deliberately took more time to develop her spare-time activities – those which would replace office work when the time came for her to retire completely. These interests centred mainly around voluntary work – she became a governor of two schools for handicapped children and a voluntary inspector of several children's homes run by a local authority.

'Most of my friends and social contacts were made through work. What we did was a way of life – it wasn't something you left behind when you left the office. When you lose work you lose the opportunity of making friendly acquaintances, some of whom could turn into real friends. You make friends at work, but most of them don't live near you. I now see very little of the people I used to work with. I had thought that some of the younger ones who I had been very closely linked with would have shown me some interest or affection apart from work. I sometimes go three or four days without seeing anyone I want to see – someone to have some sort of stimulation from.'

Meg lives alone in a flat in central London not far from a park and other amenities. But her mobility is restricted by a bad leg and she has no transport of her own. Sometimes she has to make a real effort to go out. The voluntary work is an incentive – sometimes she goes out for that in weather that otherwise would have kept her in. Recently she was invited to a college dinner and as the guests arrived they were introduced to the others by the host. Meg recalls with wry humour how this was done: 'This is Mr X who does so-and-so. This is Dr Y who is a something or other. When it came to my turn the host said "And this is Meg who ... er ... " He couldn't describe my job because I didn't have any. To him it was as if I had no identity.'

Meg admits that there are times when she is lonely. On the days when she goes out or has visitors she is content to relax on her own in the evening. But on other days she would like someone to drop in after dinner for a chat. It used to be different when she was working full-time – then it was a nuisance if a neighbour called in during the evening. Her present pattern of life is slower than it used to be and this has its pros and cons. She can take her time going round the shops and travelling wider afield than she used to. Compared with the past, she doesn't do many different things, but now does them at different times, for example, going to the launderette on a weekday instead of having to 'clutter up' a weekend. She finds her present lifestyle more relaxed and less stressful. But on the negative side evenings can be a problem. 'I find the evenings a bit sterile because now I usually finish all the things I want to do quite early, and that means I've got a very long evening ahead.'

Meg is selective about her social contacts. She doesn't spend much time with the neighbours. Her block of flats contains mostly single people, many of whom are elderly. 'I'm tired of listening to illnesses and about how terrible someone's husband was. I've heard it all before a thousand times. If I visit people like that, I do it as a service to *them*.'

She finds the general attitude of social workers and suchlike to the elderly somewhat irksome. 'Retirement makes you conscious of the fact that you are 60. Officials start treating you as an old person with all the disadvantages that entails. They assume you're deaf, dull-witted, and so on, not because you're 60 but because you're retired. It seems they like to treat older people in a childlike way.'

Meg is soon going to lose part of her voluntary work because of an administrative decision concerning the cuts in official expenditure. But she already has plans to replace the voluntary work she will lose, because one of the things she wants most is a 'regular commitment'. She has things to fill in her time – she likes puzzles and crosswords among other things – but she wants to fill that time in her own way. She sums up her main aim quite simply: 'I'd like to match my wits . . . '

(4) *Jean*

Jean has been retired for less than a year and is a young 68. Married, with two children and one grandchild, she had a variety of jobs during her working life, mostly in factories, and finished up as a sorter in the post office. A few months ago she had to give this up because of arthritis in her shoulder and neck. Her husband had retired from his job on the railway a year or so before, when he reached pension age, and his health is not too good. He stays indoors most of the time and is passive by nature, but Jean is more active and likes to get out as much as she can.

'I gave up my last job because I was ill and not because I didn't want to do it. It got to be too much of a strain. I'd be back at work tomorrow if I had the health and strength. I was very unhappy when I realised I just couldn't carry on. For the first few weeks I didn't know what to do with myself. The money was difficult, too – we had to cut out buying things we wanted. I can't do too much heavy work indoors, so we have to have a home help.'

Despite her arthritis, Jean believes in being as active as she can, both physically and mentally. 'To keep busy is the main stay of retirement, to be interested in different things. I go to the day centre twice a week and I'm on the committee there. I make toys there and do knitting for myself and for other people. I can't sit idle, so I do a bit of shopping and make little cakes. Luckily I've got good neighbours – on one side she's out all day and I've got her keys to let the gas and electricity men in, and she comes in for a chat sometimes.'

Jean speaks very highly of the day centre and the opportunities it gives her to do things and be involved with other people. 'Those kind of places, they're godsends. You can make friends there to make up for the ones you might have lost when you gave up work. There are all sorts of things you can do so there's no need to feel bored. All things considered, I think they look after the old people very well – certainly much better than they did in the old days.'

Jean's philosophy for handling retirement is a mixture of self-help, doing things and looking on the bright side. 'It's up to us to help ourselves, really. Some retired people are always saying they've got time on their hands, but I never feel this. There's always something to do. I suppose I was a bit of a fish out of water when I first retired, but I soon got that sorted out. I still see two of my old friends from work and I've made other friends at the centre. I'm retired but I'm not finished. The important thing is to keep your mind going. You can spend some of your time thinking of days gone by, but you don't want to do that all the time. Of course, if you haven't got a husband or a wife you can get lonely, but even then life is what you make it. You can go out and help other people and forget your troubles that way.'

These four very different case studies show something of the varied ways in which retirement can be faced and handled. They also help to throw light on how adequate some of the theoretical approaches to retirement are. If one thinks in terms of disengagement or activity then three out of the four are primarily activists and only Arthur is 'disengaged' (but wishing he was not – though he was never particularly engaged in earlier life, except to a work routine). Norman approached retirement with zest and had the financial resources to make himself a 'new life activist'. Meg took care to develop alternative non-work interests as she saw her employment coming to an end – she might be called a 'prepared activist'. Jean, like Arthur, did not want to retire, but carried her philosophy of keeping occupied into retirement – she is a 'busy activist'.

Three of the four were in fact retired against their wishes – Meg and Arthur because of their employers' policy and Jean because of ill-health. Only Norman chose to retire when he did –and arguably he is the happiest and most fulfilled of the four. Norman was a willing voluntary retiree, Arthur and Jean were both reluctant retirees, Arthur involuntarily and Jean voluntarily (though the decision was really forced on her by ill-health).

Different types of transition to retirement were represented among the four. Arthur was fully and arbitrarily retired at a fixed age, Norman was fully and willingly retired at a time he chose, Meg tapered off by working a year part-time before retirement, while Jean took a different and less demanding job on her road to retirement. Norman shows how full and fairly sudden retirement can work out well with an adventurous approach, but Arthur, with fewer financial and personal resources and a more rigid commitment to work routines, has fared badly by comparison. If Meg had not been able to taper off her employment, she would probably have had greater difficulty in coping with retirement than she did, since she shared with Arthur a strong, though more flexible, commitment to work. Jean's retirement from a job less demanding than her previous one was followed by a further transition to non-employment work activities such as making toys and cakes.

Our four people also show different lifestyles based on

51

different attitudes and motivations. Following Riesman (1954), we see that Norman exemplifies the autonomous type: he shows psychological self-renewal in retirement and is certainly enjoying life with no loss of spontaneity. Meg and Jean are both aptly described as adjusted, Meg mainly as a result of her preparing for retirement and Jean because of her active behaviour and optimistic nature. But Arthur must be put in the anomic category, as he is protected from the emptiness of retirement neither by inner resources nor by work connections or social relationships.

Brief accounts of four people's attitudes to, and experiences in, retirement cannot encompass the full range of retirement meanings and possibilities nor can they be representative of the retired population in general. In terms of work status and financial resources in retirement, there are many more Arthurs and Jeans than there are Normans and Megs. But the accounts can give us some indication of the range of retirement meanings and possibilities. They can also show how at least some of the different theoretical types of retirement and of retired person can be related to each other and be exemplified in the lives of real people.

The Disengagement Theory

This influential theory was first propounded by two American gerontologists, Cumming and Henry (1961). The central tenet of their theory was that, 'Disengagement is an inevitable process in which many of the relationships between a person and other members of society are severed, and those remaining are altered in quality'. As part of the theory, they put forward a number of postulates. These included a prediction that, with the expectation of death and probable decrement of ability, a mutual severing of ties will take place between a person and others in his society. When both the individual and society are ready for disengagement, complete disengagement is said to result. When the individual is ready and society is not, a disjunction between the expectations of the individual and the members of his social system results, but usually engagement continues. When society is ready and the individual is not, the result of the disjunction is usually disengagement.

The disengagement theory sees mandatory retirement at a fixed age as society's specification for when the old may become fully disengaged (parallel to the age of consent, when the young may become fully engaged). It is a theory which tacitly advocates the fitting of the individual to the 'needs' of society, since Cumming and Henry assert that fixed-age retirement 'operates even when it does not seem particularly appropriate'. Supporters of the concept of disengagement argue that it can be satisfying for the individual to disengage in retirement from some of the pressures of the world and that such an attitude is a component of successful ageing. There is, of course, a political implication of disengagement. As Estes (1978) points out, it endorses the lessened political involvement of old people and discourages them from pursuing age-related political goals.

The disengagement theory has found many supporters and an even greater number of critics. A good deal of research has been carried out to test the theory and the results of other research have been interpreted in the light of it. Cumming and Henry claim to have developed their theory in order to fit their data, which were derived from 130 older middle-class men and women in Kansas City. Much of the criticism of the theory has revolved around the point that what may be true of this particular population may well not be true of older people elsewhere and in other circumstances. Against this, Streib (1968) claims that studies made in rural Ireland and France offer evidence for the universality of the theory.

By far the greatest amount of research on disengagement has been directed at the assumption that it is at the same time universal, inevitable and functional, and the results generally indicate that it is certainly not universal or inevitable and only sometimes functional (Atchley, 1971a). A number of pieces of research do not accord with the main propositions of the theory, partly or wholly. Lehr and Dreher (1969), in their study of the determinants of attitudes to retirement, explicitly note that their results with the age group 70–75 years contradict the disengagement theory, 'happiness with retirement is solely dependent upon the experience of the present situation in the private sphere'. A. M. Rose (1965) found that his data contradicted the thesis that older people inevitably disengage. In particular, those ageing people who are conscious of belonging to a group become increasingly engaged as they pass retirement age. Lipman and Smith (1968) used a morale scale as an index of functionality and concluded that high morale was related to engagement rather than disengagement, regardless of variations in age, sex, income, health, or race.

Prasad (1964) conducted a mail survey among 900 industrial workers and found no corroboration for what he called the retirement postulate of the disengagement theory, namely that most men are ready to disengage on retirement. Among the 200 members of an Age Center in New England, there was little evidence supporting the concept of a voluntary withdrawal of the older person (Zborowski, 1962). He noted that if the pattern of living of older people had been oriented to activity and social participation, they will tend to maintain it despite chronological age and the attitudes of society.

Some studies have proceeded from a rejection of the universality of disengagement and have instead sought to determine to what extent it may be applicable to particular groups. Havighurst and DeVries (1969) surveyed the lifestyles and free-time activities of retired teachers and industrial workers and concluded that teachers maintain their engagement in the work role and in other formal associational roles decisively more often than do steelworkers. However, Havighurst and DeVries emphasise that steelworkers were not markedly engaged in most social roles even before they retired, so it was not a matter of their 'disengaging' at retirement other than from the work role.

A cross-national study carried out by Neugarten and Havighurst (Havighurst *et al.*, 1969) shows that the level of social interaction of elderly people varies not only from occupation to occupation but also from country to country. Data from Chicago, Milan, Warsaw, Nijmegen, Vienna and Bonn suggests that a general process of disengagement is probably associated with advancing age beyond 70, but the rate of disengagement and the pattern it takes is by no means the same from group to group. Significantly, the authors add that 'in group after group

... psychological well-being is positively related to the level of social interaction'.

Evidence from the Duke University Geriatrics Project (Maddox, 1965) also suggests that maintenance of activity is typically a positive correlate of satisfaction, throwing doubt on the inference sometimes drawn from the disengagement theory that activity can decrease in the elderly without loss of morale.

Consideration of the extensive body of research which fails to confirm the disengagement theory as originally formulated by Cumming and Henry (1961) has led to two developments: the spelling out of the inadequacies of the theory by its critics, and attempts by its supporters to meet those inadequacies by revising the theory. One of its foremost critics, A. M. Rose (1964) notes three points: (1) disengagement in later life is not inevitable: non-engagement during those years is simply a continuation of a life-long (or at least long-term) social psychological characteristic of some people, (2) the value-judgement that disengagement is desirable for older people is open to question, and (3) when disengagement is analysed in a context of the social structure and social trends, the theory is found to be a poor interpretation of the facts. In support of this last point, Brehm (1968) argues that psychological disengagement may be conditioned in important ways by social disengagement. In functionalist terms, it may suit 'society' that some people should disengage and they are encouraged to believe that it is inevitable that they feel it appropriate to do so.

Hochschild (1975) has criticised the disengagement theory and made a constructive proposal to meet that criticism, at least in part. He suggests that the theory is made up of a number of different components which may vary independently (for example, the individual's wish to withdraw and society's facilitation of the withdrawal process) and that it does not check with the subjective experience of many people who cannot be dismissed as simply 'failures' at disengagement. He consequently proposes that disengagement be seen as a variable rather than as an inevitable process and that studies be conducted of the conditions under which some old people prefer to disengage and others prefer not to do so.

The importance of treating disengagement as a variable

rather than as a given is also emphasised by Maddox (1968). The theory as originally formulated tended to disregard variations in the constraints of the social environment and in the patterns of the experience of individuals. To imply, as does the disengagement theory, that retirement is a single experience with a predictable consequence serves no useful purpose. That disengagement applies to some older individuals need not be doubted; that it is inapplicable to others is also apparent. The need is to specify and seek to measure the factors which account for this variation (Maddox, 1964).

Some studies of retirement have specifically focused on the extent to which, and the conditions under which, disengagement occurs. One example is the research by Crawford (1971, 1972*a*, 1972*b*) based on ninety-nine elderly people in an urban area of south-west England. He concluded that the men who viewed retirement favourably did so because they could see some chance to deny the disengagement imposed by retirement by re-engaging in the social system in a variety of new ways; this was particularly true of non-manual workers (and no doubt true also of those in relatively good health). Many of the others either had no idea what to do or intended to continue in the role of worker – to them, evidently, disengagement was very hard to accept.

Tallmer and Kutner (1969) made a study of 180 older men and women, both working and retired, using research methods similar to those of Cumming and Henry. They concluded that 'disengagement among the aged can be predicted to occur as a concomitant of physical or social stresses which profoundly affect the manner in which the life pattern of the person is redirected'. It is not age which produces disengagement but the impact of physical and social stress, which may be expected to increase with age. Disengagement is accounted for by emotional 'assaults' occurring over time such as widowhood, retirement and poor health. It is not just the passage of time but what happens to the individual that is important. Those who were highly engaged at the age of 40 tended to be still engaged in later life, and those who were withdrawn earlier were more withdrawn as they aged (Tallmer, 1967).

One way in which disengagement may be treated as a (dependent) variable is to see what independent variables appear to influence it. Thus Roman and Taietz (1967) put forward the concept of 'opportunity structures' to explain the relatively low level of disengagement among emeritus professors. These people, unlike those in many other jobs, are able to preserve a post-retirement status with a flexible work role. The university provides an organisation which facilitates continued occupational engagement. The authors suggest the possibility of improving the predictive power of the disengagement theory by incorporating an intervening variable of opportunity structures, 'intervening' presumably in the sense of being between individual predispositions and the state of being disengaged or engaged.

Two decades before Cumming and Henry put forward their disengagement theory, Queen and Gruener (1940) had proposed a theory of 'non-participation' which, in the words of one critic, anticipated all that was accurate and sound about disengagement theory while avoiding the bedevilling functionalist claims of the latter (Cowgill, 1976). Queen and Gruener argued that, while social participation does tend to decline with advancing years, it is not a uniform or universal process, there is no inevitability about it, and indeed there is great variability in the timing and extent of withdrawal. Some people carry on with little change in the extent of their involvement well into old age, while others experience sudden and severe decrements. To these authors successful ageing was not disengagement; on the contrary, it was active, pleasurable, useful participation. Non-participation was pathological at any age.

To sum up on the disengagement theory, this was first put forward as an essentially functionalist contribution to the understanding of why some people tend to withdraw from involvement with others and with society as they get older. Based on a relatively small sample of a limited population who may have exhibited 'disengagement' to an above-average degree, the theory in its original form either ignored, or sought to treat as deviants, the substantial number of people who are able, willing and happy to remain involved in the life of the community. Subsequent revisions to the theory have mitigated its unjustifiable claims to inevitability and universality, and the emphasis of later research on treating disengagement as a

57

variable and discovering its correlates has produced some useful results and promises more in the future.

The Activity Theory

Briefly, the activity theory assumes that in order to adjust successfully in retirement to the loss of one's job, one must find a substitute for whatever personal goals the job was used to achieve (Atchley, 1976). In contrast to disengagement, the activity theory postulates that successful and contented ageing depends on the older individual's integration in society, on the contribution he continues to make, and on his feeling of being still useful and needed (Rhee, 1974).

Activity theory is quite often referred to without the preceding definite article, since it has been developed fairly informally and is not attributable mainly to any one author or small group. There are several contributory strands in its development – medical, sociological, psychological and philosophical. In socio-medical terms, it has been suggested that the maintenance of high activity levels is necessary in order to inhibit deteriorative age changes in the individual and to increase his satisfaction with life (Kleemeier, 1964). Perhaps because it makes no claims to universality or inevitability, activity theory has found few challengers on a theoretical level, although some researchers have reported that the theory does not fit their results. First, however, we shall consider those studies which lend support to the theory.

Havighurst, Neugarten and Tobin (1964*a*, 1964*b*) inquired into disengagement and activity among a sample of 159 men and women aged 50–90 in Kansas City, the same location as used in the survey by Cumming and Henry to develop their disengagement theory. Havighurst found that

> as men and women move beyond age 70 in a modern, industrialized community like Kansas City, they regret the drop in role activity that occurs in their lives. At the same time, most older persons accept this drop as an inevitable accompaniment of growing old; and they succeed in maintaining a sense

of self-worth and a sense of satisfaction with past and present life as a whole. Other older persons are less successful in resolving these conflicting elements – not only do they have strong negative affect regarding losses in activity, but the present losses weigh heavily and are accompanied by a dissatisfaction with past and present life.

The more positive side of the picture is that the authors also found that those older people who maintained relatively high levels of social interaction were those who were highest in life satisfaction.

Another longitudinal study by Maddox (1963) came to similar conclusions. Among a sample of non-institutionalised men and women aged 60 and over, reported activity was found to be a positive correlate of morals. Activity but not morale tended to decrease with age, but the decline in activity was mostly in interpersonal relationships. High socio-economic status was associated with high activity and high morale.

A rather different test of the activity theory is the extent to which new forms of activity can revitalise older people. Szewczuk (1966) took a small sample of older people who, in a previous survey, had given the feeling of futility as the main reason for dissatisfaction with life. Therapy included attempts to engage these people in a new form of interest such as establishing an apiary or writing an autobiography. Eleven of the thirteen subjects showed an evident gain in self-respect and alertness, and recovery from depression. The author concluded: 'Inaction is not a necessary and irreversible phenomenon of old age; preservation of normal activity depends on the conviction of one's usefulness to others, and engagement in new forms of activity facilitates adjustment to the general process of ageing.'

Some researchers either set out with the intention of studying activity in old people generally or seek to examine activity theory in particular contexts. An example of the former approach is Beveridge's (1980) research among 185 male managers some six months after their retirement in the London area. He found that, while activity was not directly associated with retirement 'at a substantial level of significance', it seemed nevertheless to contribute to two aspects of life significance: life purpose and life interest. Two earlier studies were more explicitly concerned with the activity theory. Knapp (1977) took fifty-one men and women aged 62–86 in the south of England as his subjects. He found informal activity with friends, relatives and neighbours and formal activity (such as participation in voluntary associations) to be associated with life satisfaction, but not solitary activity such as leisure pursuits. This is in line with the findings of Lemon and his colleagues (1972) who studied movers to a retirement community in California and concluded that only social activity with friends was in any way related to life satisfaction.

One neglected area for research is the meaning of activity in later life. Although the literature is practically unanimous in its condemnation of inactivity in retirement, we know little about whether the activities of retired persons are expressions of conformity, flights from anxiety, or emotional fulfilments. Probably these and other explanations all play a part, but it would certainly be worth finding out whether different meanings, as well as levels of activity, are attributable mainly to comparatively unalterable variations in personality or whether the differences arise more from particular types of environment and social experience.

Like disengagement, activity theory is more a theory of optimal ageing than of retirement. Proponents of activity theory have not made extravagant claims, it has consequently not provoked a great deal of critical reaction, and much empirical data lend support to general propositions about the beneficial effects of continued activity in old age. In particular, seeking to replace job-specific activities with more general work activities, or to replace the latter with acceptable non-work activities, is a central element in activity theory. Activities carried out in company with others seem more important in promoting life satisfaction than do solitary pursuits.

Other Theories

Although the disengagement and activity theories and their variants dominate the field, a number of other theories have been put forward to explain aspects of the process of retirement and adjustment to it. These theories include continuity, substitution, accommodation, compromise/negotiation and functional theory. More general theories which have been adapted to throw light on processes of ageing and retirement (but which we shall not deal with in detail) include dispriviIeged minority, subculture and exchange theories (Baum and Baum, 1980).

(1) *Continuity theory* assumes that, wherever possible, the individual will cope with retirement by increasing the time he spends in roles he already plays rather than by finding new roles to play (Atchley, 1976). This assumption is based on the finding that old people tend to stick with tried and true patterns of behaviour rather than to experiment, and on the assumption that most people want their life in retirement to be as much like their previous life as possible. The continuity theory is consistent with both activity theory and the modified forms of disengagement theory, since it allows both a gradual reduction in overall activity and the persistence of some specific activity into the retirement period.

(2) *Substitution theory* is a life-stage theory in which a set of post-retirement activities is presumed to substitute for a set of pre-retirement activities and in which the measurement of adjustment is how well the post-retirement activities fulfil the same needs as the pre-retirement activities (Shanas, 1972). Substitution theory is consistent with activity theory, since the underlying need for fulfilling activities is seen to persist into old age and only the form of these activities is expected to change.

(3) *Accommodation theory* views adjustment to retirement as a process in which the individual after retirement achieves a new distribution of his energies in new roles and modes of behaviour (Shanas, 1972). The keynote is flexibility, although this theory can come close to disengagement in cases where the individual accommodates to society's withdrawal from him by developing suitably withdrawn 'roles' (almost a contradiction in terms) and withdrawn modes of behaviour.

61

(4) *Compromise/negotiation theory* has been proposed by Atchley (1976) as synthesising the major elements of disengagement and activity theories. The compromise part of the theory relates to the hierarchy of personal goals which people have. These goals are of three kinds: those we are taught, those held by others we seek to emulate, and those which grow out of our own experience. If a person's major goals are non-work oriented (such as being a decent, honest person, improving himself through reading, and so on) then little or no internal compromise may be required on retirement. But others who place work-oriented goals high on their list face the difficult task of re-ordering their priorities. The negotiation part of the theory refers to the individual discussing his goals and aspirations with the people he interacts with. In this way the social world of the individual interacts with his internal world. The results of internal compromise lead to feedback from significant others, or perhaps the other way round: in either case it is a dialectical process. Atchley admits that his theory has not been tested by research, but it seems to be a thoughtful and plausible contribution to our understanding of the process of adjustment to retirement.

(5) *Functional theory* directs attention to the 'needs' of society which are served by the institution of retirement (Breen, 1963). Functional theory in relation to retirement, as indeed functional theory generally, is based on the highly questionable assumption that society itself has 'needs' apart from those of the individuals and groups which compose it. The cold and uncaring language of the functionalist describes some of these needs: 'Retirement from work serves a useful social function in an era when labour supply exceeds demand. Retirement removes people from the work force ... it eliminates the need to retain workers whose knowledge and skills may be outdated' (Huyck, 1974). The functional view of retirement is consistent with both the disengagement theory and the history of retirement practices and attitudes considered in the first chapter: all owe more to a concern with the 'needs' of the economy than with the needs of people.

Conclusion

There are as yet no widely recognised theories of retirement, although various theories of the ageing process have implications for our understanding of retirement. It is a highly complex phenomenon which needs the insights of several disciplines: biological, psychological, sociological, cultural – and political. It should be studied in interaction with other institutions in the social system: retirement decisions are influenced by retirement policies, economic conditions, and personal characteristics and attitudes.

The two main relevant theories are of disengagement and activity. Originally disengagement implied an inevitable and universal process of mutual withdrawal of the ageing individual and society. The theory has been extensively criticised, especially in regard to the claim of universality, and a more tenable hypothesis is to treat disengagement as a variable and measure the extent to which different people and groups actually disengage.

The other main theory of activity postulates that successful and contented ageing means continuing some sort of useful role in society. Advocates of the theory have made no claims about universality, although there is a substantial amount of research evidence pointing to the beneficial effects to the individual of continued activity in later life. Other theories, such as continuity and substitution, are consistent in some degree with either or both of the main theories. No theory is politically neutral: the disengagement and functional theories, in particular, have served to support the *status quo* by subjugating human needs to the 'needs' of the economy.

3

Preparation for Retirement

What are the attitudes to work and retirement held by people who see themselves as nearing the age at which they are likely to have the choice or compulsion to retire? Some workers look forward eagerly to retirement, some want to postpone it as long as possible, while many have mixed feelings about it. Attitudes to retirement seem to depend on a number of factors such as closeness to retirement age, degree of job satisfaction, and socio-economic status.

Preparation for retirement can take many forms and can occur at varying lengths of time before the event itself. Most observers agree that to leave preparation until the worker is about to retire is usually too late for that preparation to be effective. The other extreme of starting to prepare for retirement before even entering one's first job is a semi-serious suggestion which serves to make the point that it is never too early to seek to equip oneself with the means of coping with a drastic and sometimes catastrophic change in one's pattern of life. Many people are in danger of not enjoying retirement because they give no thought to it until it is upon them.

Preference for Continued Working or Retirement

We may first examine the changes in attitude towards work and retirement which have taken place in industrial societies in the recent past. The evidence suggests that, as compared with twenty or thirty years ago, more people today are happy to retire rather than go on working, if they can afford to do so. However, a substantial minority of both men and women would prefer to go on working if they had the choice, and the reasons are not always financial.

64

There are no data for Britain which show changes over time in preferences for continued working or retirement. But American data point in the direction of a greater willingness to retire than in the past. In a study of steelworkers, Ash (1966) noted that retirement was justified in 1951 only if the individual was physically unable to continue. But by 1960 retirement was more often being justified as a reward for a lifetime of work. Thus for increasing numbers of people the concept of retirement had changed from something to be avoided to a sought-after reward. Not only had the meaning of retirement changed among these workers, but also the desire to retire had apparently increased, at least in the USA. In 1951, 57 per cent of steelworkers wanted to continue working after pension age, but by 1960 this had fallen to 35 per cent. The figure today is no doubt even lower, especially in companies which operate reasonably generous pension schemes.

In a national survey carried out in Britain in 1976 it was reported that, of all non-workers who had ever worked, 46 per cent of men and 37 per cent of women would have liked to go on working (Hunt, 1978). Despite any increase that may have taken place in the numbers willing to retire, it is clear that those wanting to go on working still constitute a very substantial minority and, in the case of men giving up work before state pension age, probably a small majority.

Surveys encourage people to give simple answers to questions which have for good reasons to be worded simply. But these answers may conceal a much more complex and often sensitive set of attitudes and reactions to experience. Case studies, such as those of Clark and Anderson (1967), help us to understand the range of feelings involved in attitudes to retirement. One retiree may be particularly indignant at being thrust into a non-worker status and complain of not getting an equal chance with middle-aged men to get a job. Another is more passive and hopeless: 'When I see all those young men at the employment department, I can tell that an old man like me doesn't have much of a chance . . .' Some recognise that their illness or disability justifies their being retired. Others more or less philosophically accept the culturally defined category of retired person. For yet others the prospect of retirement appears to be a blessing: 'Now

is the time to do all the things you wanted to do all your life.'
How often and how far these hopes and expectations are realised
we shall see later.

The Prospect of Retirement

Retirement from work is a dream to some, a nightmare to others.
Many people think that they will enjoy their time in retirement,
but when it comes it may fail to satisfy, at least after an initial
'honeymoon' period. Others are luckier – they have prepared
themselves for the change in their lives or they may be tempera-
mentally suited to retirement. Some men, tired out after an
exhausting yet satisfying life revolving around work, are anxious
to relax in retirement with all the strains relieved; others resent
the prospect of being 'put on the scrap heap' and seek alternative
outlets for their energies and alternative sources of satisfaction
or income that employment provided.

It is possible to glean from the available research findings a
number of clues to explain some of the differences in attitude,
though the conclusions are not always consistent. Jacobson
(1974*b*) notes that earlier investigators found that female
workers tended to have a more favourable attitude towards
retirement than male workers. It was thought that withdrawal
from employment to complete domesticity did not have the same
profound significance, and was a far less threatening experience,
for older women than it was for men. However, Jacobson's own
inquiry (1971) among industrial workers in their 50s showed
that the women tended to view retirement less favourably than
did the men. Only 41 per cent of the women, as against 62 per
cent of the men, preferred to retire at the pensionable age. About
63 per cent of the total sample would have opted to continue
work on a part-time basis had it been feasible in their firms.
Jacobson remarked that for both sexes a favourable orientation
towards retirement appeared to reflect constraints or resigna-
tion rather than choice. Primarily, retirement was associated
with awareness of a declining state of health, with tiredness and
with the strains and pressures of the work situation. Positive
expectations of retirement seems at best to fulfil a secondary or
supportive role. Reluctance among men to retire was associated

with anticipated deprivations, mainly of money rather than of attachment to work. Among women, on the other hand, work-based friendships were the main reason for not wanting to retire. Jacobson (1972*a*) also found that among those workers whose jobs entailed heavy strain 82 per cent were willing to retire at the pensionable age, compared with only 39 per cent of those whose jobs entailed only light strain.

In a survey among 2,700 men and women over pension age, Age Concern (1974) found that 31 per cent did not agree at all that they felt happy to retire. This constitutes a substantial number of people who were not looking forward to their new way of life. Among the retired who wanted a paid job, more than half said they were not happy to retire.

The general picture emerging from the research considered so far is that retirement is becoming more and more accepted as a fate in store for workers reaching pension age, but that a substantial minority would prefer to go on working, at least part-time. More light has recently been thrown on prior attitudes, and indeed on many other aspects of retirement in Britain, by the results of an official survey carried out in 1977 (Parker, 1980). A representative cross-section of older workers (men aged 55–72 and women 50–72) were asked what they thought about the prospect of retirement: 35 per cent said they were looking forward to it, 11 per cent were not happy about the prospect, and 45 per cent had mixed feelings. Fewer of the women than the men were looking forward to retirement, and over half of them had mixed feelings about it.

It is easy to use findings such as these to claim that most people are reasonably happy about the prospect of retirement, despite perhaps some misgivings about what it will bring; few appear to be definitely unhappy. A similarly complacent attitude is sometimes taken to the results of simple job-satisfaction surveys, which usually show that something like 80 per cent of workers are either very or fairly satisfied with their jobs. Against this, it may be pointed out that 'satisfaction' does not mean very much unless it is related to some expected standard (which may be very low) and that many people find it psychologically more bearable to be 'satisfied' than to express to an interviewer their real doubts and unhappiness about the situation facing them.

67

This probably applies to the prospect of retirement. Even if we assume that all the 35 per cent who said they were looking forward to it had no worries at all about it (a fairly dubious assumption), the fact that more than half expressed some concern should give *us* cause for concern. In response to another question, 27 per cent said they thought they would have some problems when they retired, and by far the most common problem anticipated was shortage of money. Nearly a third of the men thought they would have problems, although the figure was lower for women (23 per cent). After money, the most common problems anticipated were boredom or loneliness.

Influences on Attitudes

It seems that with increasing age the aversion to retirement grows. From his study of 2,100 males, C. L. Rose (1974) concluded that 'as one gets older and closer to retirement, desire to stave it off increases'. As a generalisation, one might say that when retirement is still a few years away it is looked forward to, but when it is very close the desire to continue working often increases. Some findings on mortality support this contention. In their study of workers in the rubber industry, Haynes, McMichael and Kupper (1974) found 'unusual increases in mortality in the two years preceding retirement'. Awareness that the undesired event of retirement was imminent would help to explain this.

According to Lehr and Dreher (1969), it appears that the attitude to retirement is dependent on a number of factors: age, previous work career, present work and family situation, outlook on the future, and certain personality traits. They suggest that for those a few years away from retirement what they call the 'immediate occupational situation' is the decisive factor. For those closer to retirement it is more often a matter of where they think they have got to in their occupational life. Whereas success seems to make it easier to retire, vocational difficulties, failures and mistakes seem to make retirement more difficult, at least in the contemporary USA. As long as someone feels that he can 'make good', he is probably motivated to continue working. For those who subscribe to the 'success' ideology, it is only when all reasonable hope of achieving success has been abandoned that retirement can be contemplated with equanimity and even relief.

Support is lent to this thesis by the research of Hall (1960), who found that most younger executives wanted to leave at the normal retirement age to pursue hobbies and recreational-cultural activities, whereas most older executives wanted to continue and often equated retirement with loss of prestige. Also, from their longitudinal study in Boston, Rose and Mogey (1972) found that as employees got older they tended to see themselves in a higher rank and therefore in a more favourable position in the company, and they preferred to stave off retirement to a later age. This thesis would also account for the change in sources of satisfaction as one gets older: there is a shift from the 'motivators' in middle age to the 'hygienes' in the pre-retirement period (Saleh, 1964). Motivators are for making further progress; hygienes (or environmental factors), the absence of which could lead to dissatisfaction, are for being as comfortable as possible in a stable, and perhaps deteriorating, situation.

It is a fairly obvious hypothesis that workers who get little or no satisfaction from their jobs will probably look more favourably on the prospect of retirement than will those who find their jobs satisfying. There seems to be a certain amount of evidence in favour of this hypothesis (Saleh and Otis, 1963). Other research, however, suggests that the relationship between job satisfaction and retirement is more complex.

Goudy, Powers and Keith (1975) outline four types of relationship between work satisfaction and retirement attitudes. First, there are people who have positive attitudes to both work and retirement: some highly satisfied workers view retirement favourably because they both like their work and feel that they can switch to enjoying leisure in retirement. Then there are the dissatisfied workers who view retirement favourably: these are the ones who are actually waiting for retirement and wish it could come sooner. For those satisfied workers who view retirement negatively it is often that they want to remain active and they see retirement as a period of enforced idleness. Finally, the dissatisfied worker who does not relish the idea of retirement may feel that work is a more significant life area than non-work, even though he is unhappy with his particular job.

From their study in a large food-processing plant, Johnson and Strother (1962) concluded that job satisfaction is not incompatible with a favourable attitude to retirement. But those whose chief source of job satisfaction stems from the work itself, as opposed to the social values of work, are less favourably disposed towards retirement. It seems that those people for whom work has the most positive values will also be those most successful in finding positive values in retirement. Just as spillover is a more marked characteristic than compensation in the relationship between work and leisure (Parker *et al.*, 1981) so it is with the relationship between work and retirement.

The meaning of work in itself is less important in determining attitudes to retirement than one might have supposed. The worker's appraisal of his present situation and the kind of experience he expects to encounter in retirement are much more important than the meaning of work *per se*. A study by Fillenbaum (1971*b*) among non-academic employees at a university and medical centre showed a very limited relationship between job attitude and retirement attitude. However, it must be allowed that among those for whom work occupies the central and organising principle in their lives, the relationship between work attitudes and retirement attitudes is likely to be stronger.

There is little doubt that prior attitudes to retirement are strongly influenced by socio-economic position. The prospect of retirement with a good pension, adequate savings and the opportunity to continue doing a chosen kind of work or to pursue other and perhaps costly interests must be very different from the prospect of being suddenly cut off from the experience and income of poorly paid employment, even though the particular job is not liked very much. The favourable case is well illustrated in a study by Ginzberg and Herma (1964) of a sample of academics awarded a fellowship by a major university for graduate or professional study. Although most of them expected to 'retire', two-thirds indicated that they would continue to engage in activities closely related to their work, for example to continue writing after stopping teaching. High socio-economic status does not have to be associated with strong work involvement to lead to a satisfying retirement, as we saw in the previous chapter in the case of Norman, the ex-director with several new retirement interests.

The view of retirement as at least to some degree a chosen extension of work or 'occupied' life reflects the favourable situation of many individuals in professional and managerial positions. Even if these people do not welcome or plan for retirement, their experience of it is usually favourable. But this does not seem to apply to most manual workers. Fleming (1962) concluded from his study of workers in the Sheffield cutlery industry that three-quarters of the men aged 55 or over were not looking forward to retirement. The fact that more than half of these men said that what they would miss most would be the company of their workmates reinforces the point that for many workers their employment is more than just a job to go to – it is an important part of their sense of identity and social life and one which they have no desire to lose. The minority who were looking forward to retirement probably had a generally low orientation to work, which would tend to keep down any resistance they might have felt towards retirement.

Table 3.1

Would/did miss most –	Workers	Retired
	(in percentages)	
the money the job brings in	48	31
the people at work	24	36
the feeling of being useful	10	10
the work itself	8	11
things happening around	3	5
the respect of others	2	3
other answers	5	4

On the subject of things that people think they will miss most when they retire, the survey quoted earlier (Parker, 1980) revealed that, although money comes top of the list, half of those interviewed thought they would most miss things other than money, notably the people at work. Table 3.1 gives the answers of a representative cross-section of workers in all industries, within ten years of state pension age. These answers are compared with those of retired persons who were asked what they actually did miss. After retirement, many of those interviewed found that they missed the people at work more than the money, and this particularly applied to women.

A few years previously, Atkinson (1970) made some claims which the survey broadly substantiated in spirit, if not statistically:

> . . . if any serious thought is given beforehand to what retirement will mean, it will be about the sudden and serious drop in income. Very few give thought to any other aspect of their future pattern of living. If the same people are asked six months after their retirement what they have missed most since they ceased to work, the vast majority will admit that they miss their colleagues and the work, the companionship and purposeful activity. Money matters have dropped to about fourth on their list. Very few had realised beforehand to what extent they were dependent on their colleagues at work for their day-to-day companionship. Very few had realised beforehand the extent to which the discipline, routine and sense of purpose in work had governed their day and given them satisfaction.

Money has not receded as a problem for most retirees to quite the extent that Atkinson supposed. Nevertheless, it is clear that for many people much else besides money is lost when the job is given up and that the non-monetary losses tend not to be anticipated.

The general picture that emerges of prior attitudes to retirement is that more people are having to recognise that it is a fate in store for them, whether they like it or not. How attractive or unacceptable retirement appears to be to any given individual depends on a number of factors: his attitude to work, the degree of success or fulfilment he has achieved, his expected income in retirement, his interests apart from work, his opportunities for preferred work after 'retirement', his health, his domestic situation, and so on. There is evidence that financial deprivation in retirement is fairly widely and realistically anticipated, but that other deprivations become more apparent only after the event.

Types of Preparation

There are four different sets of people or agencies who can play a part in preparation for retirement: (1) the institutions of further education, (2) employers, (3) special agencies (public or charitable), and (4) employees themselves. We shall look at each of these in turn, to see in what ways and with what degree of success they have been tackling the problem. Although trade unions may be thought to constitute a fifth possible agency of preparation for retirement, their role is in fact negligible in this respect, although their role in negotiating for early retirement and better conditions for their retired members is more substantial.

The Role of Education
The role of the institutions of further education in preparation for retirement takes two main forms, one of which may be regarded as direct and the other indirect. On the one hand, a still small but increasing number of employers are encouraging, or at least allowing, their older employees to attend courses at colleges and similar institutions, sometimes on a day-release basis. The aim of these courses is to provide practical advice and information on how to cope with the problems of retirement, and there is a substantial supporting literature serving broadly the same purpose, of which the books in Britain by Mossman (1971), Miller (1978), and Kemp and Buttle (1979) may be cited as examples.

On the other hand, older workers may prepare for retirement by attending courses which teach skills or offer the opportunity to practise activities to occupy their time in retirement, as many will need an absorbing interest to help fill that time. The crafts and hobbies centres set up by the Glasgow Education Department are an example of this type of provision (Anderson, 1969).

Education has a valuable role to play in retirement preparation because of the wider horizons which it can open up for older people. As noted in the Russell Report on adult education (Department of Education and Science, 1973), preparation for the conclusion of a working career is an important facet of the process by which education can assist in setting work in a meaningful relationship with a whole life. Provided that the individual has not been worn out by work, and has a positive rather than a negative concept of life after employment ceases, retirement may well occur at a very 'teachable' time for many (Taylor, 1972). To compensate for the losses in activity, social contacts and feelings of usefulness, the retired person may turn to some form of education as a means of personal growth.

The Role of Employers
Some employers regard it as part of their responsibility towards older and probably long-serving employees to take various steps to prepare them for retirement. The proportion of employers taking such steps is difficult to determine. One survey a few years ago found that pre-retirement courses or seminars were organised by 19 per cent of the companies studied, but only 8 per cent of managers had the opportunity to attend such courses (Smith, 1974). The proportion of managerial staff attending pre-retirement courses is much higher than that of manual and less senior white-collar employees. The recent official survey of retirement found that only 2 per cent of a general sample of older workers and the retired had been on any kind of pre-retirement course (Parker, 1980). Furthermore, it seems that most courses are geared to retirement *at* state pension age rather than before or after, since 7 per cent of persons who retired at that age had been on a course.

The situation in other industrial societies is probably similar. A recent survey in Western Australia showed that only 2·8 per cent of retired persons and 3·7 per cent of the pre-retired had attended any talks or meetings to help in preparation for retirement (Donovan and Associates Pty Ltd, 1978). It does seem, however, that some types of employee, particularly white-collar and professional, are more likely to have the opportunity of

74

attending pre-retirement courses than others: for example, 25 per cent of white-collar women in a Midwestern state survey said that their employer offered a regular, formal pre-retirement programme, and 32 per cent of that number attended (Prentis, 1980).

In many cases what is done by employers is very minimal: an informal chat by a manager on, or a short while before, the day of retirement, and covering little more than the pension plan and perhaps answering other questions if asked. Only a minority of employers in Britain appear to have organised anything resembling a set of preparation for retirement measures. One such firm is the Hepworth & Grandage engineering works in Bradford, whose programme includes individual counselling, a preparatory series of lectures on retirement, a gradual process of paid leave as a means of phasing out, and information packages – all taking place during the final year of employment before retirement (*Age Concern Today*, 1974).

Another firm which has helped to pioneer retirement preparation courses is Rubery Owen (Rainsbury, 1970). Believing that adequate preparation is a long-term process that calls for concentrated application throughout ten or fifteen years, the firm started such a scheme in 1958. By trial and error it has been learned how best to retain the interest of people who participate in the scheme. Refresher courses held at five-yearly intervals were found to be poorly attended and of little value. Instead an evening class in simple household repairs and decorations was set up: after sixteen weeks the class remained together as an interested unit and its members were keen to go on learning more. No doubt the combination of sociability and doing something useful and interesting was the key to success.

Griffiths (1973) gives further examples of what employers are doing in this respect, and he suggests that the motive for these measures may be better public relations: 'Anything that is seen by the employees as being done to help prepare for the shock of retirement, and as continuing that concern after retirement, will inevitably improve their attitude towards their employers, and will therefore be reflected in performance at work and in the greater financial stability of the firm concerned.' Efforts to minimise the shock of retirement, despite the ulterior motive suggested, are undoubtedly worthwhile, but the same cannot be said for employers' 'concern' for their workers after retirement. Given adequate preparation, once the break is made it may be better to keep it that way. For example, revisiting the workplace may be a sign of difficulty in adjusting to retirement. Whether the retiree wants to be visited occasionally or frequently in his home by ex-workmates is a different matter and open to personal preference.

It should not be assumed that the same kind of retirement programme is appropriate to all types of employee. Interest in taking part in a retirement programme seems to vary inversely with occupational status: one US study showed that 65 per cent of a lower-status group were interested, 50 per cent of a middle-status group, but only 17 per cent of an upper-status group (Fillenbaum, 1971*b*). Also, the higher the occupational status, the greater the likelihood that retirement plans have been made. It is as though the worse someone's position, the more he worries about retirement, but the less he actually does anything about it, partly no doubt because of limited opportunities for appropriate action.

It is one thing for a work organisation to have a programme to prepare its employees for retirement, but quite another thing to know whether that programme is effective in achieving its aims. A small number of research projects have been designed and carried out to test the efficacy of various types of programme, of which the project reported by Glamser and DeJong (1975) may be cited. The group discussion programme was found to be effective in increasing knowledge of retirement issues: participants felt better prepared for retirement, they evidenced less uncertainty about the future, and were more able to make plans. But the effectiveness of the individual briefing programme was relatively minimal.

Christrup and Thurman (1973) came to a similar conclusion with regard to the features of the pre-retirement programme in a Washington federal agency. Factual presentations by guest speakers in a large auditorium and the distribution of published materials were found to be far less effective than informal meetings in small groups with maximum involvement by participants who were encouraged to discuss their psychological and emotional feelings about retirement as a prelude to planning for their retirement years.

It seems that the success of pre-retirement courses in generating more favourable attitudes to retirement cannot always be taken for granted. The average worker's tendency to ignore the need for planning may be too strong to permit him to benefit from the pre-retirement counselling and training. It has even been suggested that some pre-retirement programmes may do more harm than good (Kent, 1965). They may arouse anxiety about retirement without preparing the individual to cope either with the real problems of those conjured up in the class. The very attempt to help someone to overcome the expected difficulties, by way of retirement education schemes, may only serve to emphasise the difficulties to him. Also, it is questionable whether counselling is best given before rather than after the event. According to Pyron and Manion (1973) there is very little difference in the adjustment of retirees who participate in pre-retirement as compared with post-retirement counselling.

It appears that, although many people say pre-retirement courses are helpful, few can point to any real change they have made as a result of attending a course (Beveridge, 1980). There is a danger that the balance of the course may present those problems which can be dealt with easily during the course rather than those which are important during retirement. The strong emphasis in many courses on environmental issues such as housing and finance may lead some retirees to imagine that these are the only issues that matter. A greater emphasis seems to be needed to enable retired people to see the creative possibilities ahead of them. A series of talks given by experts in finance, home maintenance, hobbies, health, and the like are not likely to meet the need to come to terms with the deeper meaning of life in retirement. Beveridge suggests two desirable steps: the selection and training of course tutors who are able to undertake a counselling approach, and the limitation of course numbers to a size which allows for easier and more open discussion.

Very few pre-retirement courses attempt to tackle in any depth the psychological aspects of the transition from work to retirement. But the achievement of an adequate philosophy of life in retirement is the most important theme that should run

77

though the whole pre-retirement process. With this in mind, Pasterfield (1981) advocates pre-retirement groups that encourage the members themselves to ask the questions and seek the answers as they must do in retirement. This approach is essentially one of active participation rather than passive instruction. Instead of experts at a top table, there are participants at a round table.

The Role of Agencies

A third source of retirement preparation measures consists of various public or charitable agencies. There are several bodies in Britain which are concerned wholly or partly with the problems of retirement: among these are Age Concern, Help the Aged, and the Pre-Retirement Association. Each of these bodies publishes literature which is designed to help individuals cope, either before or after the event, with life in retirement. At a local level, voluntary organisations such as Retirement Councils, Old People's Welfare Associations and local authority Citizen's Advice Bureaux also play a part.

It is fair to say, however, that the retirement preparation function of all these agencies is essentially a responsive one, and that many men and women who could in fact benefit from information, advice or help do not at present seek it. This has led to suggestions that more might be done by way of developing a new social service, on 'marriage guidance' or 'citizen's advice' lines, for those about to retire, and to extend existing pre-retirement courses to make it possible for groups of men and women about to retire to become actively identified with each other and their needs and to pool their resources (Crawford, 1973).

Self-Preparation

Finally, and most importantly, there is what the person facing retirement can do for himself. It is all too easy for retirement, if not prepared for, to be simply a period of uselessness and dependency between regular employment and death. But retirement can be a time for taking up new and useful activities and interests, and adequate provision needs to be made for this kind of retirement.

Most scholars of ageing and its problems are agreed that preparation for successful or contented old age starts early in life and that the way a person reacts to retirement corresponds to his reactions to earlier events and phases of life. A significant variable is type of occupation which, in turn, is linked with educational level and with characteristic attitudes or sets of values. From one study of hourly wage-earners in the USA it was concluded that 'while recognizing and anticipating financial problems at the time of retirement, their planning efforts are limited by a lack of information and technical planning expertise' (Morrison, 1975). Relevant information sources and planning expertise are more likely to be available to those in jobs at higher socio-economic levels, although this does not necessarily mean that the eligible people will take advantage of facilities available to them.

Whether retirement is voluntary or compulsory is another important influence on preparation. In a survey of men recently retired from large US companies it was found that 72 per cent of voluntary retirees had made plans, compared with only 40 per cent of those who had retired compulsorily (Kimmel, Price and Walker, 1978).

The recent British inquiry showed that about one in six of those who retired under pension age said they would like more information, advice, or help about retirement. The kind of information most often wanted was about the state benefits they were entitled to and advice about leisure and recreation (Parker, 1980). According to Simpson, Back and McKinney (1966). 'middle-status' workers were the group most likely to seek advice about retirement. Lower-status workers were thought to be unaccustomed to the idea of seeking advice, while higher-status workers probably felt they did not need to.

One controversial question is whether planning actually helps adjustment in retirement or not. It is easy to assume that it does, but the act of planning itself does not necessarily make up for other inadequacies in preparation for retirement. One of the main conclusions from the Cornell Study of Occupational Retirement was that planning for retirement is largely unimportant to good adjustment in retirement (Shanas, 1958). Favourable pre-retirement attitudes and a realistic appraisal of the retirement situation was found to be more important in facilitating good adjustment.

Conclusion

More people today than in the past want to retire, but substantial numbers still want to go on working. Attitudes to retirement vary according to a number of influences, including socio-economic level, how close people are to retirement, and how successful their working life has been. Financial deprivation in retirement is widely anticipated but other deprivations, such as missing the people at work, are not.

Although we have considered preparation for retirement under several different headings of bodies promoting the preparation, it would be wrong to suppose that these are alternatives. While from the standpoint of the individual some benefits may accrue from pursuing one type of preparation without the others, from the standpoint of society as a whole what is really needed is a concerted programme involving all possible approaches. As Anderson (1970) suggests, future policies must be developed to increase opportunities for adult retraining; to provide preparation for retirement courses to promote a full or at least satisfying life after employment ceases; to set up centres for hobbies and crafts where creative and useful activities can be arranged; to make re-employment bureaux available for part-time or full-time work; and to stimulate the growth of retired employees' associations to provide security and prevent loneliness. Not all retired persons will need all of these facilities, but many will need at least one.

The most effective forms of preparation for retirement are those which rely on participative 'round table' group sessions rather than purely instructive 'top table' lectures. It is important to go beyond mundane issues such as housing and finance to the vital question of the achievement of an adequate philosophy of life in retirement, and indeed of life preceding retirement.

4

The Capacity of Older People to Work

One of the reasons – but by no means the only reason – which helps to explain why we have such an institution as retirement is the common belief that beyond a certain age most people become unfit for work. From the employer's point of view, it is often claimed to be uneconomic to employ older people. There is, of course, some justification for seeing the elderly, in general, as slower and less energetic than younger people: common observation tells us that older folk usually walk slower and are not so often found in the top range of most sports. But the claim that older men and women are generally unfit for work needs much closer scrutiny.

Until recently, a substantial proportion of men and women over pension age were in fact employed either full-time or (mostly) part-time, and even today the numbers are not negligible. No one suggests that the health of the elderly has got worse, resulting in their reduced capacity for work. Rather, what has happened is that, while the capacity for work has probably remained unchanged or may even have improved (thanks to better medical and social services for the elderly) the opportunities and perhaps the motivation for work have diminished.

In this chapter we shall review what is known about the physical and psychological capacities of older people for work, the productivity and general satisfactoriness of older workers, and the implications of these considerations for employment policies. The chapter concludes with some general remarks about the theory and social context of work and the elderly.

Physical Changes and Capacities

Viewed in purely physical terms, the ageing process does have an adverse effect on a person's ability to perform various actions.

The successive changes of bodily, including neural, structure which take place between birth and old age are clearly such that, if the human organism is seen as a piece of anatomical and physiological machinery, it rises to a peak of efficiency in the early 20s and thereafter slowly declines (Welford, 1958). But work is not merely a matter of the human body acting as a machine. Human activity (including though not limited to work) is better conceived as a composite of physical, mental and social action. What often happens with increasing age is a redistribution of the individual's time between these three types of action – the proportion of physical action tends to be reduced in the lives of most people as they grow older (Havighurst, 1961).

Sometimes physical changes with advancing age do reduce capacity for activity to the point where employment of any kind is impossible. But such cases are the exception rather than the rule, at least during the years immediately following the conventional retirement age. Very large numbers of men aged 65 and over are in sufficiently good health to be able to work. A US survey carried out in the mid-1960s (Rosenfeld and Waldman, 1967; see also Jaffe, 1972) found that only half of the men reported themselves as suffering from chronic conditions which prevented the carrying on of work activities; the other half reported themselves as being physically capable of working. Yet of this latter group three in five were retired. Earlier, a medical study in Britain had shown that 86 per cent of men aged 65–69 were fit for work of some kind (Brown, McKeown and Whitfield, 1958).

Another measure of (mainly) physical ability to work is days lost from employment because of incapacity. According to Logan (1953) the proportion of elderly men who do not have any incapacity is almost as great as for younger men. The figures for working days lost because of incapacity actually showed a falling off after the age of 65, but this was probably because a greater proportion of those in poor health took the opportunity of retiring at pension age.

Psychological Changes and Capacities

Advancing age is usually accompanied by certain psychological changes, but the onset of these changes is usually gradual. Also, there is an unfortunate tendency to label losses of some mental abilities in such a way as to imply that they are characteristic of increasing age: a lapse of memory is said to be a sign of senility in an older person, but a comparable lapse in a younger one is dismissed as mere forgetfulness.

There is no reason to believe that mental or emotional impairment is much more widespread among the elderly than among the young. Indeed, there is some evidence of a decline in the rate of mental disorder after the age of 70; neuroses and some psychoses tend to 'burn themselves out' with age. However, there is a more general problem of the decreased capacity of older people to cope with what Belbin (1953) calls time stress in industry, though this affects employability only in certain kinds of job where speed is at a premium, not employability generally.

Some research and much discussion has centred on whether you can 'teach an old dog new tricks'. According to Jarvik and Cohen (1973) older learners differ from young learners in that they tend to respond more slowly, are more sensitive to interference while engaged in a learning task, and often show a decline in immediate and short-term memory. But they are by no means ineducable. In fact, they surpass young learners in verbal and integrating ability. Also Glenn (1969) tested the hypothesis that as individuals age they become less likely to hold or to express opinions, and concluded that available evidence provided no support for this hypothesis.

One of the most serious difficulties faced by older people is society's definition of what men and women are, and can do, in retirement. Older people – like the rest of us – are subject to social and psychological pressures which influence their view of themselves and what they feel capable of doing. This process of labelling means that older people's capacity to work is often underestimated, and the elderly themselves find it difficult to resist accepting that unduly low estimation.

Productivity in Different Kinds of Work

In considering the capacity of older people to work, the crucial question is not whether ageing brings about changes which affect employment opportunities and abilities generally, but how effectively older people actually perform in specific types of work. A good deal of research has been carried out on quite well-defined, if narrow, aspects of older people's working abilities, for example, changes in their nervous system, in their vision and hearing, their reaction times and their ability to cope with environmental changes. In what follows I shall review the findings of some broader studies which relate either to productivity, in general, or to achievements in particular fields of work.

Surveys made to determine the relative productivity of workers of different ages usually find that output remains rather stable through the mid-50s with a slight falling off thereafter. Results vary somewhat with the type of job. Women office workers, for example, show little change in output over the whole employed span. In one experimental investigation there were no age differences in production between groups of factory workers, even though psychomotor test performances did fall off with age in the same subjects (Chown and Heron, 1965). In another investigation, the older subjects were found to be less efficient than the younger subjects only at the highest and lowest rates of work they performed, the most probable explanation being the poorer co-ordination of the older subjects (Norris and Shock, 1955).

A survey of older workers' efficiency in jobs of various types suggested that working speed does seem consistently to decrease with age (Smith, 1953). However, an increase in efficiency with age was reported for the unskilled group, with a concomitant increase in co-operativeness, steadiness and attendance. Johnston (1955) also found elderly workers to be extremely conscientious: 'they are excellent time-keepers, they start work promptly at the appointed hour, need the minimum of supervision, and work right up to the normal finishing time.'

Heron (1960) reported that in a survey of twenty large firms in British manufacturing industry many managers and foremen referred to 'slowing-up' between the ages of 51 and 65. But when account was taken of the changes for the better that were mentioned, there was a slight balance of favour of the older men. In attitudes, personality and general behaviour they were regarded as superior to younger workers. Such adjectives as responsible, reliable, conscientious, tolerant, reasonable, loyal were frequently used. There was also an improvement with age in labour turnover, timekeeping and absenteeism. Breckinridge (1953) paints a similar picture of elderly workers in the USA. Representatives of many companies pointed out that age made very little difference in office and clerical jobs. One company found older people to be more reliable, not only as clerks and guards, but also in some skilled occupations. Another company wanted older workers for jobs requiring attention and conscientiousness.

The situation in France with respect to older workers seems to be similar to that in Britain and the USA. Daric (1955) reported that, in general, for the different industries and different types of worker, output begins to decrease from the age of 50. For skilled workers the fall is especially marked from the age of about 60 in the metal, engineering and electrical industries, and from the age of about 65 in building. But commercial, administrative and supervisory staff between the ages of 50 and 59 show a definitely higher and better quality output than that of younger workers. Sickness absenteeism was lower among workers aged 50–59 than among younger workers, and this was especially true of skilled workers. However, from the age of 60 onwards sickness absence was more frequent in all categories.

What is true of many factory and most office occupations seems also to apply generally to professional and artistic occupations. One knows, of course, about the exceptionally talented individuals who continue their celebrated careers into their 80s and even their 90s, but surveys involving wider samples of older people are not so well known. Thus Cole (1979) found that there was no decline in the quality of work produced by mathematicians as they progressed through their careers. Both a slight increase in productivity through the 30s and a slight decrease in productivity over the age of 50 are explained by the operation of the scientific reward system. Dennis (1966) made a study of the total number of works produced by over 700 individuals in scholarship, the sciences and the arts who lived to be at least 79. He concluded that, for scholars as a whole, the 70s were as productive as the 40s. Literary activity follows a similar pattern. Lehman (1953) showed that the total range for 'best production' extended from age 22 to 80, and for quantity of output – good, bad and indifferent – the production rate was almost constant from 30 to 70.

Employment in relation to Capacities

It is one thing to be able to show that productivity is, by and large, affected only minimally, if at all, by age, and quite another thing to ensure that unfounded prejudices about ageing held by employers and others do not unfairly reduce employment opportunities for the elderly. Ageing has been alleged to reduce employability in several different ways: (1) physical: loss of strength and endurance, loss of co-ordination, decreased vision and hearing; (2) temperamental: irritability, poor relationships with others, increased emotionality; (3) cognitive: difficulty in learning and with short-term memory; and (4) personality: changes in self-image, loss of confidence, suspiciousness, reluctance to adapt (Stagner, 1971). The short answer to these claims is that some elderly workers do show some of these changes some of the time, but it is relatively rare for a particular individual to show all such changes. Some people are very effective in compensating for particular handicaps or shortcomings and, as already noted above, they tend to have certain other qualities and attributes which younger people do not have, or have to a lesser degree.

Manual work is the type most often cited as being less suitable for older workers because of their reduced strength and endurance. In previous years the proportion of heavy work in industry was high; the number of men on this type of work declined after about the age of 50, and with this move from heavy work there was frequently a reduction in skill. But in most jobs today the physical demands are well below the capacities of most older workers. Some years ago Clark (1955) studied the problems of ageing in the building industry. He concluded that the industry as a whole was fairly well adapted to give elderly men a chance of remaining in employment, provided they are carefully distributed throughout the full range of building jobs and contracts.

86

In other industries, technological developments have replaced jobs which formerly required physical strength and endurance with jobs where machines do this kind of work under human guidance and control.

Older workers seeking new employment face even greater difficulties than those whose problem is how to avoid losing their existing jobs. Employers seem to feel that the older workers they already have are for the most part satisfactory, but they tend to look upon older workers seeking new jobs as a poor employment risk, even though this view is not supported by evidence such as that quoted above. If older workers are properly placed, they function effectively and have greater stability on the job, fewer accidents and less time lost from work than younger workers (Meier and Kerr, 1976).

We may conclude that there is no justification for an arbitrary and rigid retirement policy applied at 65, or indeed at any age, on the grounds that beyond that age service would be so punctuated by incapacity as to make it unprofitable for it to continue. Though continued employment after late middle age is probably undesirable in those diminishing number of occupations which impose a heavy physical burden on the worker, this is not the case for the majority of occupations. Provided the elderly can, where necessary, be relieved of some of the load they previously carried, there seems no reason why they should not keep on working if they wish until their own individual states of health render it expedient that they should stop.

One unfortunate consequence of compulsory retirement is that, for those who try unsuccessfully to find further work, the ensuing period of unemployment may mean a deterioration of skills and a gradual acceptance of the unemployed status, which combine to reduce employability. This experience parallels that of many younger unemployed workers. There is some justification in the claim that unemployment is worse for people too young to enter the ranks of even the early retired and probably with family responsibilities, than it is for older people reaching or past 'normal' retiring age. But unemployment at any age is still unemployment, and at an advanced age it must often seem like finally being thrown on the scrap heap, a phrase which reluctant retirees often use about themselves.

87

Conclusion

In this chapter we have been considering general propositions about the capacity of older people to work, either at all or in particular occupations, and the evidence for those propositions. But we must remember that there are wide variations in individual capacities to work. Indeed, research has shown that the variation among individuals increases as the age of people studied increases. Older people are individuals and their attributes should be judged as such. A scatter-graph of older people's capacities shows a wide overlap, up to the highest-levels of capacity, with those of younger people (Fogarty, 1975).

At the risk of formulating further generalisations which mask individual differences, it is worth following Jones (1976) in outlining two contrasting theories about ageing and capacity to work. One commonly conceived syndrome of creeping and irreversible decline in physical and intellectual capacity, a decline based on physiological loss and degeneration, might be termed theory A. Many of the administratively convenient customs and practices in the employment and retirement of older workers are implicitly based on this theory. By contrast, theory B, while not denying that some changes with age affect some types of employment adversely, emphasises that, in the absence of pathological destruction, much of the reduction in capacity is not inevitable. In short, getting old *per se* is not a disease. Theory B accounts for much deterioration in terms of lack of use or exercise, and its supporters claim that the use of a faculty extends its life and can enhance it.

It may readily be conceded that ageing usually means some loss of strength and speed, and that jobs which place a premium on such attributes are better left to younger people. But if we consider work in the wider sense of useful activity, there is no need to be defeatist about the role of the elderly. In the words of Cicero (quoted in Cooley, 1965): 'People who declare that there are no activities for old age are speaking beside the point . . . Great deeds are not done by strength or speed or physique; they are the products of thought and character and judgment. And far from diminishing, such qualities actually increase with age.'

5

The Experience of Retirement

In most industrial societies the average age of retirement from paid work is tending to come down. In a few countries the age at which people can draw their full state retirement pension has been lowered, for example from 65 to 62 in the USA in 1972. Provision has also been made in some cases to facilitate 'early' retirement by offering reduced pensions at ages below those at which the full pension would be payable. An increasing number of employers are providing their own pension schemes under which employees can be encouraged to retire with two pensions at normal pension age or with the single occupational pension (sometimes boosted by a lump-sum payment) at an earlier age.

In this chapter we first consider the various reasons that people have for retiring, both 'early' and at or after normal retirement age. Then we look at what happens to people when they retire: how far and in what ways they adjust, the problems they face, the meanings they find in retirement, its effect on their health, morale and sense of identity, and finally what wives think of their husbands' retirement.

Reasons for Retiring Early

People are said to retire early if they do so before the age at which most employees in their industry or firm are entitled to draw an occupational pension, or before state pension age, whichever is the earlier. In Britain the current state pension ages are 65 for men and 60 for women, but men in some jobs, for example civil servants, are entitled to draw a full occupational pension at 60, provided they have accumulated enough years of service.

Surveys of early retirement fall into two main groups: those of cross-sections of the whole early retiring population, and those of selected categories of early retirees, usually individuals quitting work on decidedly more favourable terms than the average. Results from these two types of survey are quite different, so we shall take the 'selected population' inquiries first.

McGoldrick and Cooper (1980) carried out what purported to be a 'study on the decision process and experience of the British early retiree'. It was based on questionnaires and interviews with 120 male early retirees and their wives from companies based in the north-west of England. The main reasons given by this sample for early retirement were 'finances right', 'worked long enough/deserved retirement' and 'wanted more free time'. Health accounted for only 10 per cent of all reasons given – not surprisingly, as 'early retirements through complete disability/ill-health were generally excluded from the sample'. Because, as we shall see below, ill-health is a major factor in early retirement, the McGoldrick and Cooper sample cannot be taken as representative of the general run of early retirement in Britain. The finding that 'the majority are satisfied with the early retirement experience' is thus open to question.

A national study of early retirement from 180 companies was carried out at the University of Oregon in 1968. Among the findings was that 75 per cent of the early retirements were said to be 'voluntary' (though these included 7 per cent who were too ill to work) and that almost four-fifths of all those retiring early had looked forward to doing so (Heidbreder, 1972). But because of the way the study was structured, all of the men surveyed were receiving pensions from their former employers and in addition 85 per cent were receiving other income. They were not, therefore, representative of all early retirees in the USA.

The same applies to a study by Owen and Belzung (1967) of manpower reduction at an oil refinery in Texas. The informants were 454 men aged 50–64. The men generally seemed to be enjoying their early retirement status: only three in ten regretted their retirement and wanted to keep on working. Two in five saw no disadvantages in early retirement, while less than one in ten saw no advantages. But, again, in interpreting these findings it must be taken into account that the company concerned had a particularly generous early retirement plan: for example, a worker could retire at 55 and get 72 per cent of his pension due at 65.

Turning now to more representative national surveys, we may take first the one carried out in Britain in 1977 (Parker, 1980). From that inquiry it is clear that many early retirees – particularly men – are forced to give up work against their wishes for reasons of health. No less than 76 per cent of men who had retired under state pension age reported that they had some illness or disability which handicapped them or interfered with their activities in some way, and 50 per cent of men retiring early gave ill-health as the main reason. Furthermore, 44 per cent were sorry that they had retired (the average for all retirees saying this was 21 per cent). Although there has been a growth in 'administrative' early retirement since that survey was carried out, there is no reason to suppose that the current figures for early retirement due to ill-health have come down much below the high 1977 level.

Similar findings have been obtained from properly representative inquiries in the USA. In reporting findings from a survey of new social security beneficiaries in 1968, Reno (1971) concluded that many of the early retired employees did not want to retire, and their attitude was probably related to retirement income. About 70 per cent of men retiring at or before 65 reported that they had left their jobs because of poor health, compulsory retirement, loss of jobs, or poor returns on their business. Most of the remaining 30 per cent had been willing retirees.

Data from the national and longitudinal Retirement History Study show that 'men aged 58–63 who had withdrawn from the labour force by 1969 reported poorer financial situations than did labour force participants, and substantially more of the non-participants reported that health problems interfered with their ability to work. More than half had been without work three years or longer' (Schwab, 1974). The author comments that any notion of early retirement as added years of carefree leisure should be modified. Neither the health nor the financial situation of most men aged 58–63 who have withdrawn from the labour force supports the idea that early retirement is carefree.

Policies for early retirement often vary according to the particular occupation in which workers are engaged. Several European countries have in recent years enacted legislation designed to allow early retirement from some heavy manual jobs. For example, as long ago as 1964 regulations concerning arduous and unhealthy work were introduced in Greece which allowed for retirement five years earlier than normal retirement age if the type of work had been done for at least four-fifths of a specified qualifying period (*International Labor Review*, 1964; see also Berglind, 1978). A quite different group of men are also influenced to leave work early: those in managerial, professional and other groups who, in addition to government benefits, also receive occupational pensions and lump-sum benefits ('golden handshakes') when they leave employment as part of a policy of reducing the workforce (Daniel, 1974).

From a survey of retirement-age practices between 1960 and 1976 in ten countries, Tracy (1979) concludes that there has been no general lowering of the retirement age for the average worker. What has happened is that more workers in various categories have been allowed to retire early with full or partial occupational pensions, including workers with long service, poor health or in occupations where the employer wished to reduce the labour force.

What are we to conclude from the extensive research (the findings of which are not always consistent) which has been carried out into the extent, problems and consequences of early retirement? The similarities between Britain and USA are more marked than the differences, although it is clear that proportionately more American early retirees are financially better off than their British counterparts. Many of the apparent differences between survey results are due to selectivity in the populations sampled. Some early retirees from some companies do quite well, financially and in other respects; the picture is not nearly so bright for the majority of other early retirees.

Despite a pervasive and only slowly declining attachment to work as a source of identity, self-respect and fellowship, many older workers seem to face the prospect of early retirement with some equanimity, even delight, provided that their employer has a pension scheme which will give at the earlier retirement age a large proportion of the full pension which would be payable at normal pension age (usually 65). As against this, some people who accept – and more who are forced to accept – early retirement suffer a severe cut in their income and consequently in their standard of living. This adds to other, more psychological, losses which a number of workers suffer when they retire, notably the loss of workplace companionship and the difficulty of finding useful and interesting things to do. Furthermore, the advantages to the employer of encouraging or making workers retire early are doubtful, as is the proposition that an early retiree makes room for a younger unemployed person to take his job.

Reasons for Retiring at or after Pension Age

The term 'normal retirement' is used to mean retirement at an age when the state pension becomes payable or when the mandatory retirement age laid down by an employer comes into effect. However, it is scarcely a statistical norm as fewer than half of all retirements take place at state pension age. The British 1977 survey showed that about 48 per cent of male retirements (over a period of years) were at 65, and the comparable figure for women's retirements at 60 was less than a quarter (Parker, 1980). For the sake of convenience, I shall use 'retirement' below generally to refer to retirement at any age, but not to any special age, since early retirement has already been dealt with in the previous section.

There are quite a large number of inquiries which have been concerned with reasons for retirement and other related matters. Let us take the British studies first, followed by the American.

In 1953 the Ministry of Pensions and National Insurance (MPNI) (1954) undertook an interview survey of about 24,000 men and women who were eligible to receive state retirement pensions. Of the 12,000 men and women reaching the minimum pension age of 65, 40 per cent took their pension and 60 per cent continued at work. The reasons given for retirement were slightly different for men retiring at

65 or at 66–70, but there was little difference between reasons given by single and married women retiring at 60 (see Table 5.1).

Table 5.1   *Reasons for Retirement*

	Men retiring		Women retiring at 60	
	at 65	at 66–70	Single	Married
		(in percentages)		
Chronic illness	25	9	15	14
Ill-health	25	38	29	31
Heaviness or strain of work	4	7	5	4
Retirement by employer or discharge	28	24	7	8
Wish for rest or leisure	7	8	8	9
Other reasons/not answered	11	14	36	34

Anderson and Cowan (1956) surveyed 323 men aged 65 and over in the Glasgow area, of whom 25 per cent were still working and the rest retired. Of the retired, 37 per cent said they did so voluntarily, 29 per cent through ill-health, and 34 per cent were compulsorily retired. When asked their reasons for voluntary retirement, about one-third said that it was because of the strain of work, one-third that it was 'time to retire' although they were fit to carry on, and a sixth were tired of work. The authors note that 'voluntary retirement may be in the nature of compulsion, owing not to the employer but to the character of the work'.

Richardson (1956) carried out a socio-medical study of 244 retired men aged 65–75 in Aberdeen. Thirty-one per cent of them had retired for reasons of health alone, and a further 16 per cent for health combined with other reasons such as pressure from the family, illness of spouse, dislike of the job, strain at work, or having sufficient income to retire; 27 per cent had retired because of action by employers; 10 per cent because of strain at work; and 7 per cent because of illness at home. In presenting these results, Richardson remarks that 'occasionally a clear-cut cause of retirement was apparent, but in the majority of cases a combination of factors had been responsible'.

In 1976–7 two national surveys were carried out which included questions on reasons for giving up work in later life (Hunt, 1978; Parker, 1980). Although the age ranges were broader in the Hunt survey, and there were differences in the ways in which the data from the two surveys were analysed, the results are broadly similar (see Table 5.2). Health is an important reason for men retiring under pension age, but less so for women. Compulsory retirement is more often the reason for men having to give up work at 65. Redundancy seems to slide into early retirement for a substantial number of men under pension age.

Table 5.2   *Reasons for giving up work (last job)*

	Men		Women	
	Under pension age	*Over pension age*	*Under pension age*	*Over pension age*
		(in percentages)		
Own health	50 (49)	12 (20)	39 (36)	27 (29)
Compulsory retirement	6 (11)	39 (42)	1 (1)	12 (15)
Redundancy	19 (22)	3 (5)	5 (6)	3 (11)

Note: The first figures are from the Parker survey and the figures in parentheses are from the Hunt survey.

Turning now to the American studies, we can see a change over the last quarter century or so in the reasons given for retirement, although the results of surveys carried out at different times and using different research methods are not easy to compare.

In a survey conducted by the US Bureau of the Census in 1952 it was found that only 13 per cent of all men aged 65 and over who were out of the labour force had retired under the rules of formal retirement systems (Gordon, 1964). An additional 11 per cent had been retired voluntarily because of age, lay-offs, or for other reasons. Gordon suggests that later figures would probably be different, and this is confirmed by Jaffe (1972) who refers to unpublished 1967–9 census data. When asked why they quit work, a cross-section of American men aged 65 and over who were not in the labour force gave mainly the conventional answer 'retirement or old age' and 34 per cent said that they did so because of personal or family reasons, ill-health, or because the job gave out. Jaffe maintains that these latter reasons probably denote involuntary retirement and that 'retirement or old age' could be either voluntary or involuntary. He concludes that perhaps half or more – certainly more than the 34 per cent mentioned above – were involuntarily retired.

A social security survey of retired persons aged 62+ carried out in 1963 showed that among men voluntary reasons (mostly a preference for leisure) were given by 31 per cent and involuntary reasons (mostly poor health) by 69 per cent (Palmore, 1971). Among women, some of whom gave more than one reason, the respective percentages were 58 and 62.

The results of an earlier national survey sponsored by the Twentieth Century Fund, and quoted by Parran *et al.* (1953), had revealed that

> 57 per cent of the persons surveyed had retired because they had reached a compulsory retirement age, and 25 per cent had retired because of poor health. The kind of occupation had apparently borne some relation to reasons for retirement, since 67 per cent of managers and executives had retired because of age and only 10 per cent for reasons of health, while 48 per cent of labourers and operatives had retired for reasons of age and 35 per cent because of health.

A survey carried out in 1951 and reported by Corson and McConnell (1956) covered sixteen business corporations, two state retirement systems and one international union. Reasons for retirement were found to be: 56 per cent company's policy on age, 26 per cent poor health, and 9 per cent to have more time to themselves. But the authors note that 'the large proportion compelled to retire because of age overstates the significance of this cause among all workers'. Age policy reasons may have been overstated in relation to the US national situation in 1951, but other evidence already cited suggests that they are not overstated in relation to the more recent past. Retirement for many occurs, in effect, because no acceptable alternative job seems to be available.

Finally, data from the ten-year Retirement History Study

show that for men leaving their last job between 62 and 67 health
was the main reason given by 28 per cent, to draw a pension by
19 per cent, and job factors by 9 per cent; for non-married
women the respective figures were 28, 15 and 10 per cent (Bixby,
1976).

Table 5.3 gives a summary of the major reasons given for
retirement in the British and US national surveys quoted above.
Unfortunately the answers were itemised in different ways and
so the comparisons are rough rather than exact.

Table 5.3   *Summary of Reasons for Retirement*

	Britain			USA		
	MPNI 1953	Hunt 1976	Parker 1977	Corson and McConnell 1951	Parran et al. 1953	Ten-year Retirement History Study 1969
				(in percentages)		
Health	50	20	29	26	25	28
Action by employer	28	47	31	56	57	9
Other	22	33	40	18	18	63

Note: Percentages are of men retiring at 65 or over, except the survey quoted by Parran *et al.* in which women were also included, and the ten-year survey in which the retirement ages were 62–67.

The relationship between state of health and retirement is a
complex one. A great deal more knowledge about the health and
social background of older people is needed before the answers
to questions about reasons for retirement can be fully assessed.
On the one hand, poor health may be the sole or a contributory
factor in leading to the decision to retire and, on the other hand,
a person's state of health may be affected by his experience of
retirement. Here we consider only the first question, leaving
until a later section the question of the effect of retirement on
health.

Let us look first at the evidence concerning poor health as a
reason for retirement. In the two major British national surveys
(MPNI, 1954; Parker, 1980) health figured prominently as a

reason for retirement. In the earlier study 'chronic illness' was recorded as the reason in 25 per cent of cases of retirement at the minimum pension age, and 'ill-health' in a further 25 per cent. In the later study, 'own health' was given as the main reason for only 10 per cent of retirements at minimum pension age, although the comparable figure for early retirements was 45 per cent. In both surveys men more often gave ill-health as their main reason for retirement than women (50 per cent of male early retirements in the 1977 survey).

Data from the USA gave a broadly similar picture, that is of ill-health as an important reason for retirement, but one which has been declining over the last two or three decades. In the earlier national surveys quoted above, (Corson and McConnell, 1956; Parran *et al.*, 1953) poor health accounted for 26 and 25 per cent of retirements. But census figures covering the period 1967–9 (Jaffe, 1972) show that health reasons were given for only 18 per cent of retirements.

Three trends are probably influential in accounting for this declining proportion of retirements which are attributable to poor health. One trend is the improvement in medical services and in the general standards of health of older people. Another is the changing nature of the occupational structure: fewer jobs require hard physical work which, in turn, demands physical fitness, and more jobs can be done by those whose state of health would previously have caused them to retire. But perhaps most important of all is the growth of 'administrative' retirement: more people in relatively good health are being retired for reasons connected with the needs of the employer or with what are supposed to be the 'needs' of society rather than with their own inclination in the matter.

Adjustment to Retirement

With retirement come important and sometimes unfortunate changes in a person's circumstances. Income is reduced, often drastically, he or she is cut off from friends at work and (particularly for a man) his status in his family may change. At worst, retirees become poor and lonely; at best, the rhythm of their lives is broken. However, the picture is brighter for others, for whom retirement brings relief from burdensome responsibilities, freedom from the demands of employers and the pressures of work and routine. For these people it can be a chance for a new life.

A good deal of the literature on different ways in which people experience retirement is concerned with how well or badly they adjust to it. The word 'adjust' is seldom defined, but it seems to have at least three shades of meaning. First, it can denote *satisfaction* or happiness, a fairly positive feeling that retirement is good and perhaps better than expected. Secondly, it can mean *adapting* to changed circumstances, deliberately altering one's behaviour and attitudes in order to cope with a novel situation. Thirdly, there is the more passive idea of *settling down*, which implies quiescence on a new basis after an event or period of upheaval.

Although studies of work satisfaction show that it tends to increase with advancing age, this does not hold for satisfaction with retirement. Many retirees under 65 report low satisfaction, because their retirement is freqently due to ill-health; satisfaction with retirement increases at the age of 65 and then decreases consistently with age (Price, Walker and Kimmel, 1979). Another study concluded that men who had been retired for less than five years were more satisfied than those who had been retired for longer than five years (Kerckhoff, 1964).

One measure of adjustment to retirement is how people rate it relative to their previous state of being employed. The recent British national survey showed that about equal proportions of those who retired under pension age were glad or sorry that they had retired (many of them had to retire because of ill-health), more who retired over pension age were glad, and even more of those who retired in their year of reaching pension age (Parker, 1980).

Socio-economic status and consequent level of income is very important in influencing satisfaction with, or adjustment to, retirement. Satisfaction with retirement life is substantially correlated with an adequate financial situation (Friedmann and Orbach, 1974), but some research among managerial retirees suggests that, although not to have enough money almost certainly guarantees dissatisfaction, having enough money does not necessarily provide satisfaction (Beveridge, 1980).

People in different socio-economic groups are affected differentially by factors, such as leisure opportunities or exposure to information about retirement, which themselves make for good adjustment. Many men in managerial jobs have difficulty in accepting retirement and adjusting to it. For someone who has sought and accepted responsibility, and for whom the job has been his main life interest, the assignment of his duties to others often leaves a void that is very difficult to fill. From their survey in Wisconsin, Draper, Lundgren and Strother (1967) concluded that, in general, the white-collar, foremen and skilled employees were more satisfied with retirement than service, semi-skilled and unskilled employees. The man or woman to whom work means many important things may have more flexibility and capacity to adjust to retirement.

Adjustment is often helped by new or continued interests. Life satisfaction has been found to be greater among retirees who become more active in various leisure pursuits than among those with constant or decreased activity levels (Peppers, 1976). A similar study of older men in California suggested that successful adjustment depends on a man's ability to carry over into retirement, interests he has maintained throughout life (Livson, 1962). Whether retirement activities are productive or useful seems less important than whether they provide continuity with the past and satisfy lifelong needs. The durability of retirement interests is much more important than their nature, because now they furnish the outlet for energies formerly given to the job.

Studies of particular groups of retired persons reveal something about the ways in which individuals adjust, or fail to adjust, to retirement in different circumstances. Those living in retirement communities often find that their own adjustment is facilitated (but in some cases impaired) by the prevailing attitudes and institutional practices of the particular community (Hoyt, 1954). It seems that married women generally face fewer problems in adjusting to retirement than most other marital status groups; on the other hand, retired single women, when compared with men in comparable types of work, show similar problems of adjustment: a feeling of being 'lost', the need to reorganise their lives, and the seeking of time-filling activities (Anderson, 1958). For the sick and disabled, retirement tends to be a gradual process, beginning when they define themselves as unable to work (or forced into unemployment against their will) and ending when they accept themselves as having retired (Blaxter, 1976). Elderly people who are made redundant often experience great difficulty in finding other employment and many have to adjust to the reality that they have, in effect, been retired prematurely.

Survey results can be used to show that most people adjust reasonably well to retirement, in the senses of adapting and settling down rather than of experiencing positive satisfaction. In the recent British national survey about a third of retired persons said they had some difficulty in settling down during their first twelve months of retirement, but most of them subsequently did so. Atchley (1975), in his study of retired teachers and telephone company employees in the USA, came to a similar conclusion: nearly a third encountered difficulty in adjusting to retirement − or, to put it another way, more than two-thirds adjusted satisfactorily. Finer measurement scales can be used to determine the degree of adjustment to retirement; for example, in Loether's (1964) study of retired Los Angeles men 49 per cent said that they had made very good adjustments and 36 per cent good adjustments. But what does this mean in terms of quality of life? The man who says that he has made a very good adjustment may, in effect, be saying no more than 'Given the situation in which I find myself, I am making out very well'. However, it is probable that, given the choice, he would prefer not to be in the situation in which he finds himself.

Finally, it may be that, although a reasonably high proportion of retirees are satisfied with their lot, people who are not retired are even more satisfied. This certainly seemed to be the case among the 6,000 older men and women surveyed by Hansen, Yoshioka, Taves and Caro (1965): 60 per cent of the fully retired preferred their status to others, 71 per cent of the partly retired, and 76 per cent of the fully employed.

Gains and Losses

For many people retirement is a mixed blessing: there are felt to be both gains and losses in the change of status and daily routines from worker to retired person. No one has made a comprehensive survey – based either on what retired people say or on an empathetic understanding of their situation – of the gains resulting from retirement. However, these are some of the main propositions which have been advanced:

(1) Retirement gives you more leisure or time to do what you want.
(2) Retirement means the end of all that is irksome about paid employment.
(3) Retirement strengthens personal relationships, especially between husbands and wives.

Let us examine each of these propositions in more detail. Retirement as more time is a gain only if that extra time formerly devoted to work or work-related commitments is used in satisfying ways. Ideally, retirement is 'the freedom to choose a way of life which, when related to character, education and opportunities, will offer the maximum contentment' (Samson, 1972). Some people are indeed able to make the best of their opportunities to spend more time on old interests or to develop new ones. But, unfortunately, as we shall see when considering retirement and leisure below, this potential freedom in retirement is by no means always realised.

If retirement as more time is essentially 'freedom to . . . ' then retirement as the end of paid employment is essentially 'freedom from . . . ' Jones (1974) lists some of these gains: 'freedom from the clock . . . , not having to keep up, freedom from taking orders . . . ' Everything which is disliked about employment is a candidate for being such a 'retirement gain': having to get up in the morning, having to put up with bad travelling conditions, doing unpleasant, boring or tiring work, having to eat canteen food, and so on. The feeling of freedom from everything connected with employment may be summed up as 'independence' and this was the most popular answer given by 40 per cent of retired London industrial workers in a survey by Beveridge (1968).

A more positive retirement gain is the opportunity it provides for husbands and wives to spend more time together and to share activities. Theoretically, other non-work relationships, such as grandparent or family counsellor, should be strengthened by the greater time available in retirement, but there is little or no research which throws light on the extent to which this actually happens.

Turning now to the losses incurred on retirement, we can see that these also fall into a number of categories:

(1)   Retirement means missing things to do with the job.
(2)   It means the loss of a functional role in society.
(3)   It brings greater awareness of a time void to fill.
(4)   It leads to less communication and hence more isolation.

Just as everything disliked about employment can be a retirement gain, so everything liked about employment can be a retirement loss. In Chapter 3 we saw that not only did workers approaching retirement think they would miss the money, the people, the feeling of being useful and the work itself, but after retirement they tended to miss the people at work even more than the money. In the survey by Beveridge quoted above, 74 per cent missed most the companionship of the workplace, 27 per cent the money, 20 per cent the job itself, and 14 per cent the routine of working life.

There is often a loss of occupational identity suffered by those who retire. To the extent that retirement is seen as an instrument by which people are removed from the labour force, those who are not prepared for this – and even some who are – will suffer a debilitating social loss. The worker who feels that he has not been successful may be quite vulnerable to the negative effects of retirement. Impending retirement signals the end of effort to move upwards, a confrontation with his own failure.

The second theme of retirement as the loss of a functional role in society is really an extension of the first. If one acceptable social role is exchanged for another then no loss may be felt. But often nothing significant replaces the occupational role: on retirement there is a formal rejection of the worker not just by the employer but also by the community. In providing people with a source of legitimate income, work also provides self-respect, companionship, supportive rituals, and intrinsic

103

interest or challenge. Although retirement may sometimes make possible alternative means of self-respect, companionship, and so on, there is no guarantee that it will do so or that the ageing individual will be sufficiently flexible to take advantage of any opportunities available. We shall return to the subject of loss of occupational identity when considering later in this chapter the consequences of retirement for morale.

Thirdly, retirement tends to bring greater awareness that there is time to fill. To the person with realistic plans for the use of extra discretionary time there is no problem, but for others time hangs heavily in retirement. One survey has shown that of men workers within ten years of pension age only 10 per cent very or fairly often had time on their hands that they did not know what to do with; among retired men in the same age group the figure was 48 per cent; the corresponding figures for women were 6 per cent and 31 per cent respectively (Parker, 1980). Shanas and her colleagues (1968) drew similar conclusions from their research in Britain, Denmark and the USA: men who continue work, compared to men who are retired, are more likely to say that they are never lonely or that time never passes slowly for them. It is also true that too much time can spoil the essential spontaneity and joy of leisure: the retired person may make a routine out of his leisure to fill the void left by the loss of routines centred about the job.

Finally, retirement often leads to less communication with others and hence to more isolation. By reducing income and disrupting the social network that mostly accompanies employment, retirement tends to isolate the individual. Unless other activities are found to fill the void left by loss of work contacts, the retired person may find it difficult to retain old friendships or make new ones, thus reducing his opportunities for communication.

The Meaning of Retirement

What are the various meanings retired people attach to their condition? Retirement may mean happiness or misery, fulfilment or frustration, novelty or boredom. It is interesting to see how the meaning of retirement tends to change from anticipation to realisation. Analysis of the answers given at the pilot stage of the recent national survey (Parker, 1980) enable the various meanings to be divided fairly crudely into positive (P) and negative (N) items. The quantitative results at the main stage of the survey showed that about two-fifths of older workers were looking forward to retirement, one in eight were definitely not happy about the prospect, and the rest had mixed feelings. The qualitative results suggest a more even balance between positive and negative feelings, which probably means that some people who put themselves in the 'mixed feelings' category in the main survey were expressing a mixture that was on balance negative.

Looking first at the answers of older workers, we can discern a number of different meanings attached to retirement. These are (in descending order of rough frequency):

(1) *A feeling of freedom and being able to please yourself* (P). This includes having no restrictions and doing what you want when you want. Some typical answers were:

> I shall be able to please myself about what I do and where I go. (Labourer, aged 62)

> Knowing that you don't have to go to work any more – having more time for shopping and that. (Woman, aged 57, machinist)

> If you want to stay in bed you can, then get up and go out for a walk if you want to. (Man, aged 56, legal executive)

(2) *Looking forward to more leisure, time for hobbies* (P). Sometimes this is related to the idea of escaping to leisure and, in other cases, the leisure activity itself is mentioned:

> It means escape from work. I think I've done enough work to get retirement. Time to open up a few years of leisure. (Fitter's mate, aged 64)

> Your life's centred on the home then. Instead of getting up to work you do what you want: dressmaking, decorating or gardening. (Manageress, aged 54)

105

> I can spend my time with my flowers in the garden. I hope to do a bit more travelling ... (Man, aged 61, compositor)

(3) *The idea of getting old* (N). A male bus driver of 62 sums it all up:

> When I've reached 65 I won't feel terribly happy about it. I don't feel I want to retire. If I wasn't well, that would be different altogether. I don't want to be old and useless and not be able to do anything. I want to be active.

This is echoed by a 55-year-old woman factory supervisor:

> Getting old, that's what it means to me. I think it makes you feel old when you retire.

(4) *Time to rest, relax, have a lazy life* (P). No doubt in many cases this is an understandable reaction to a lifetime of hard work, though in others it perhaps expresses a basically lazy nature:

> Having a damned good rest. I've never had a rest in my life. I've worked hard all my life. I've never had anyone to spoil me. (Woman, aged 59, presser)

> After all these years of work it's a rest that you're looking forward to. Let the young people take over. (Storeman, aged 65)

(5) *The end of working life* (N). These answers express sadness and regret rather than joyful anticipation:

> It means finishing work, doesn't it? It's a serious thought ... I shan't see my friends, I would miss them. (Woman, aged 57, chargehand)

> It means you're really then coming to a final stage. It makes you feel that way ... Unless you plan your life now and do things when you retire, you'll be stuck and

won't want to do anything. (School-meals supervisor, aged 55)

Other positive meanings of retirement expressed by smaller minorities of workers were: doing the things you always wanted to do, adjusting to the new life, and enjoying it. Other negative meanings were: loneliness, boredom, missing the earnings and missing the work.

Most of the above themes – particularly freedom and more time for leisure – were also voiced by at least some of the retired people interviewed. None of the retired, however, said that retirement meant getting old to them: probably they just accepted that as a fact. Other themes in the meaning of retirement emerged in their answers (again in descending order of mentions):

(1) *Retirement means poor health* (N). The survey showed that poor health is very often a reason for early retirement. Health is an important concern both for those who retire early and 'on time' or later:

> I'm retired and have to take it easy – I'm living on borrowed time now, I feel. With my heart I must take it easy or I've had it. (Ex-mason, aged 66)

> I can't say I'm happy – there's so much that I'd like to do that I'm unable to do ... I can't do much because of my state of health. (Ex-housekeeper, aged 64)

A sub-theme on the good effect of retirement on health is more positive:

> Retirement is the finest thing that ever happened. If every man retired at 65, their health would improve and they would live much longer. (Ex-boilerman, aged 68)

No doubt this is true of the physical health of many heavy manual workers, but, as we shall see below, it is much more questionable whether the mental health of other types of worker is improved by their retirement.

107

(2) *A time to enjoy life* (P).

> The idea of retirement? I don't know really – the time to enjoy yourself. You think you have time but you don't. I can always find plenty to do . . . (Ex-home help, aged 50)

> I'm living a new life, meeting different people, relaxing more and seeing more of my friends. (Ex-catering manageress, aged 62)

> I think it's great, you can mix pleasure and work – a bit of work and a lot of pleasure. (Ex-engineer, aged 71)

(3) *Something to adjust to, accept* (P). This has a positive and a negative side, the positive only just outweighing the negative:

> You come to the age when you have to retire and you just accept that . . . you wonder how you will spend your time, but honestly I'm so busy now that I sometimes wonder how I managed to find the time to go to work. (Ex-typist, aged 68)

> It means you've got to start on something different altogether and adjust to not doing as much. I've got hobbies and it doesn't bother me now. (Ex-blacksmith, aged 70)

> I'm retired compulsorily – it hit me hard, but I've learned to live with it. I've always worked and would love to have worked. (Ex-foreman, aged 66)

(4) *Feeling the loss of money* (N). Usually these are brief references to shortage of money in retirement, but sometimes there is a note of bitterness about the felt deprivation:

> Retirement means loss of income – when you have to live on a third of what you've been living on for the past 25 years. (Ex-ambulance driver, aged 70)

108

You've more time to do what you want, but not the money. (Ex-engineer, aged 71)

(5) *Nothing to do, having time on your hands* (N). This, together with the next theme of boredom, would combine to form the second most frequent negative meaning after health:

> Lazy life. I've nothing to do but go for a couple of pints twice a week. (Ex-boilermaker, aged 71)
>
> It's just having nothing to do. I've always been to work all of my life. (Ex-school-meals supervisor, aged 62)
>
> I don't like the time on my hands. (Ex-nurse, aged 68)

(6) *Boredom, being fed up* (N). A rather more 'bolshie' attitude to having nothing to do:

> It's blinking monotonous. Life is tedious when you can't do anything ... time goes slow, you get fed up with it. (Ex-stock keeper, aged 71)
>
> I have no garden and no hobbies. There are times when I get fed up – I feel I'd like to go back to work. (Ex-market trader, aged 64)

(7) *Something to dislike, even hate* (N). This broadens out to a kind of frustration that is born of an intense dislike of all that retirement stands for:

> A tragedy. I can't bear the anger of being unable to go around. I hate the thought of being an old-age pensioner – I've always been active. I hate the thought of it. (Ex-truck driver, aged 64)
>
> I hate it because I was never an idle person in my life – I've taken it badly being at home. (Ex-salesman, aged 72)

(8) *Loneliness* (N). More plaintive than hating retirement, there is an air of desperate finality about many of these answers:

> It's a lonely life. I'm here on my own and the neighbours are very quiet ... I was happier when I was working; I had a lot of friends but I haven't seen them since I finished work. (Woman, aged 70, ex-textile worker)

> When you retire it leaves a sudden gap in your life. One minute you're busy and the next you're on the shelf ... In my job I met a lot of people, getting to know them. In retirement I miss this ... (Ex-insurance man, aged 66)

(9) *Wanting a job* (N). Finally, there are those who answer the question 'What does retirement mean to you?' by saying how much they want to return to work. This desire is often coupled with one or more of the meanings given above:

> It's the firm's idea, not mine. They think you're too old to go on working. (Ex-lorry driver, aged 69)

> I haven't come to accept it yet. I keep hoping a miracle will come along and I'll be able to get another job (Ex-foreman, aged 63)

To sum up, these and other statements about the meaning of retirement leave one with the impression that the negative feelings and experiences outweigh the positive. This may be partly deceptive because it is easier perhaps to complain or be critical than to expound on the theme that things are broadly all right. But for a lot of people retirement clearly means a reduced quality of life and more deprivations than they suffered when they were still working.

Health

The relationship between retirement and health has been the subject of much study and some controversial interpretation. It is therefore necessary to weigh up all the evidence carefully, to examine critically any assumptions made, and to be prepared to draw complex conclusions. A distinction between physical and mental health – although the two are often linked – is also desirable, because their relationship with retirement is not necessarily the same.

Most of the studies that have found retirement to have a beneficial effect on health have been concerned mainly with physical health, although sometimes the references have been to health in general, which may lead one to assume that they include mental health. One of the most frequently quoted studies is by Martin and Doran (1966), of a sample of 604 men aged 55+ employed in a factory where compulsory retirement at 65 was the policy. They analysed data on the incidence of serious illness before and after retirement in two ways: (1) by comparing groups of retired men with groups of men in the last ten years of their working lives, and (2) by examining the trends over time before and after retirement. Whereas the first method led to the conclusion that there was no difference between the health of retired and working men, the second method showed a distinct drop in the incidence of serious illness in the two years following retirement and a slower rate of increase thereafter. The authors conclude that 'retirement is associated with a substantial lowering in the incidence of serious illness'.

Another major longitudinal study was carried out in the USA by Thompson and Streib (1958). This was concerned with the changing self-appraisals of health among 1,260 men workers and retirees. Both groups were about equally likely to shift in their self-rating of health, but retirees were found to be more likely to improve in health, while the employed were more likely to decline. The authors noted that because those workers in poor health tended to retire voluntarily, even though reluctantly, poor health was found relatively more often among retirees. But they thought this could best be understood in terms of poor health leading to retirement and not the reverse.

A somewhat similar survey reported by Shanas (1958) of industrial workers in large American organisations came to similar conclusions: 'Persons in poor health are more likely to retire. If any general effect at all can be discerned which relates to retirement and health, it is that retirement leads to an improvement in health.' The apparent considerable incidence of ill-health in the first year or two of retirement is perhaps due to neglected symptoms in the last years of work. Also it appears that workers themselves are likely to believe that retirement will have a positive effect on their health, at least from a physical point of view – 56 per cent of a sample of those whose jobs involved heavy strain thought this, compared with only 29 per cent of those with light strain (Jacobson, 1972*b*).

A substantially different picture emerges, however, when we look at the relationship between retirement and mental health. Far from retirement having a beneficial effect, it often seems to be harmful. Admittedly the evidence is based less often on empirical inquiry and more often on judgements or conjecture about 'cases'; and the relevant surveys are limited both in number and in scope. Crawford (1972*b*) reports a study of fifty-three married couples in Bristol: 'From the way in which subjects talked about retirement before it happened to them, and the way in which some of them described it afterwards, it did seem to be a psycho-social crisis.'

A study in San Francisco found that depression scores peaked soon after retirement, then dropped, and later rose again (Spence, 1968). However, the proportion depressed did not equal that at the initial impact of retirement until the subjects had been retired for over ten years. The increase in depression among those who had been retired more than ten years was thought to be explained by age and such age-related factors as poor physical health. It also appears that retired women are more likely to be psychiatrically impaired than retired men (Lowenthal *et al.*, 1967), although other evidence suggests that retirement is, in general, less stressful for women than for men.

Doctors and social workers undoubtedly come into contact with many people who are both retired and in a poor mental state. But social scientists are divided on the issue of whether or not retirement is to blame for bad psychological effects. Butler (1972) reports that 'the clinician sees many people for whom retirement participates in the genesis of depression, apathy and paranoid states as well as those in whom it precipitates behavioural and mood changes not of pathological dimensions'. In a similar vein, Johnson (1958) refers to a 'depressive retirement syndrome': retirement gives more time for previously latent maladjustment to come to full bloom and dominate all spheres of living. Symptoms most commonly complained of include depression, insomnia, loss of usual interests and lack of communication. Significantly, Johnson observes that persons with these retirement symptoms have usually functioned in work as passive recipients of implied approval, acceptance and appreciation.

Geist (1968) seeks to relate the symptoms of retirement depression to their causes, rooted principally in the loss of employment activities and status. There is often a decrease in memory for recent events, a kind of turning away from the painfulness of the present, a sharpening of memory for the past, especially when life was successful. Other symptoms include a more assertive attitude as a compensation for insecurity, mild depression resulting from isolation and loneliness, and increased sensitivity and anxiety caused by death among people in the same age group. A comparable analysis of neurotic symptoms was made by Cameron (1945): the retired worker misses the externally imposed routine, he loses his familiar landmarks, his points of reference, and with them his sense of personal identity. The experience of being unnecessary and unwanted may precipitate restlessness, weariness and dejection that lead to hypochondria, chronic fatigue states, or neurotic depression with resentment and self-deprecation.

In seeking an explanation of low morale among the retired it is possible to find that the actual condition of being retired is not so much to blame as other characteristics which are associated with retirement. From his survey of men aged 65+, Thompson (1973) concludes that the retired exhibit lower morale than the employed principally because they have more negative evaluations of their health, are more functionally disabled, are poorer and are older, and not simply because they are retired. Also, it is thought that the onset of mental illness after retirement is frequently preceded by a physical impairment and is more highly related to the effects of disease and to consequent social isolation than to retirement itself (Lowenthal, 1964).

However, the claim that retirement is not to blame for a substantial worsening in mental health is not entirely convincing because it seeks to separate retirement from some of its currently most obvious manifestations. It is precisely because the retired tend to be poor or to be isolated that their mental health suffers. This does seem to be recognised by quite a number of retired people themselves. Unlike the improvement in physical health which many people expect retirement to bring, it seems that a majority of men believe that compulsory retirement is detrimental both to their health (probably they were thinking mainly of their mental health) and their contentment. We must also remember that our society is one in which the gap between the most privileged and least privileged sections is large and that inequalities are additive rather than compensatory. Those who are privileged socio-economically are also privileged physically and psychologically when they retire.

Morale and Identity

There is a fine line between mental ill-health and such psychological effects of retirement as loss of morale and of a sense of personal identity. Here we shall consider those consequences of retirement which border on the pathological but which mostly enable the person affected to lead some sort of fairly normal life, emotionally unsatisfying though it may be.

The level of morale in retirement depends to a large extent on the meaning attached to life in retirement and on the satisfactions which can be derived from it. For some people retirement is a goal towards which they have been working, a culmination of years of hope and planning. For others it is a trap, a misfortune for which they are unprepared. As Friedmann and Havighurst (1954) point out, what retirement means to a person depends partly on what his work has meant to him. If he can get the satisfactions out of retirement that he formerly got out of work, or if he can get new and perhaps greater satisfactions in retirement than he got in his work, then retirement is a boon to him. In all this, the social context of individual morale must not be forgotten. Many retired people want their working status back in some form, together with a normal future-oriented life. It is not so much a matter of their being incapable of enjoying some of the things they want as there being laws and conventions preventing their access to those things.

For those who experience a loss of morale in retirement, the event and its aftermath have been variously compared to the sick role, divorce and bereavement. When a man becomes sick, he is normally expected to get better – the loss of good health is in most cases regarded as temporary. When a man retires from work rather than to a new life, the loss of work is permanent. To a large extent, the retiree's prognosis depends on the attitudes he has learned and the attitudes of the people who matter to him. To the person who has become emotionally attached to his job and the wealth of meaning, sense of achievement and identity and social contact and approval it brings, retirement can seem like compulsory divorce from a beloved spouse, an act of incredible cruelty (Wolff, 1959).

Furthermore, retirement is, in many cases, rather like bereavement, inasmuch as it creates a sense of loss. Everyone recognises that there is a loss of income and often a loss of other things connected with work, but perhaps the most important loss is that of social recognition. Employment has satisfied all these human needs, and too few people have prepared an adequate substitute. Of retired men and women in San Francisco, Clark and Anderson (1967) write:

> Many of these people seem to be in mourning, sometimes unable to recover from the loss of employment and the significant activity accompanying it . . . Sometimes the self cannot be perceived as existing outside of an occupational role . . . the unemployed self has a moribund quality. One subject could not get beyond this description of himself: 'I was a waiter *in my life.*' By clear implication his life is no more.

Reluctant retirement is not dissimilar in its effects from long-term unemployment. This particularly applies to those men, below but not far off state pension age, who lose their jobs and who, because they are unable to get other employment, slide into early retirement. Harrison (1976) writes of the demoralising experience of prolonged unemployment among older men:

> Recognising their low employability, and the need to adjust in the near future, anyway, to a retirement income, and feeling they have contributed fully to society over a long working life, they manage to maintian their self-respect, and consciously

try to adapt to a reduced income and to the altered routines of daily life. By no means all the older unemployed take this view. Many bitterly resent being 'thrown on the scrapheap' before, as they see it, their usefulness to society is exhausted ... Certainly Arthur, the retired messenger we described in Chapter 2, felt that way.

Studies by Streib (1956), Wolfbein (1963) and George (1974) confirm that, even among older persons with good health and adequate income, morale tends to be higher among the employed than the retired.

Loneliness and boredom are twin problems facing many of the retired. The old people studied by Tunstall (1966) tended to regard the absence of work – even if work was not a practical possibility – as a factor in their being often lonely. The reports of social workers concerned with retired people suggest that unhappiness in retirement is not solely attributable to ill-health or financial difficulties and that boredom, loneliness and loss of personal significance are common symptoms. When you have barely enough time to get through all your commitments, leisure is a wonderfully tantalising prospect. Yet when retirement finally brings the opportunity to develop new interests, time tends to drag for many. Boredom and lethargy frequently set in.

Problems such as morale and loneliness affect retirees to different degrees and in different ways. In the remainder of this section we shall look at the influences of sex, social class and a number of other factors on the mental experience of retirement.

In families where the husband is the breadwinner and the sole or main role of his partner is that of housewife, retirement, representing the loss of a significant life role, is likely to be a more demoralising experience for the husband than for the wife. However, for many women, particularly the single, divorced and widowed, the work role is a very large and salient component of their adult lives. Retirement from that role may leave them with few non-work-related social supports relative to women who have not been in employment or for whom part-time or temporary work has been of only financial significance. For many married couples, retirement of the husband, is in effect, a joint decision profoundly affecting the lives of both spouses, and in the section below we shall consider the attitudes of wives to their husbands' retirement.

Social class – very largely determined by type of occupation – is an important influence on the way retirement is perceived and coped with. As we saw in the section on adjustment to retirement, class is significant in offering differential access to leisure opportunities, information about activities, and related matters. Although work is generally more salient in the lives of those in middle-class occupations such as managers and professionals (as compared with working-class, manual or routine non-manual occupations), middle-class people tend to have more resources to cope with the loss of their employment which, in some cases, may not equate with loss of their particular type of work. Not surprisingly, therefore, the largest proportion of those with high morale among the elderly has been found among those still employed, in good health, and with high socio-economic status (Streib, 1956).

Cutting across social class is the urban-rural dimension. Few studies have investigated differences between city and country dwellers in coping with retirement, but there are indications that retirement is generally less traumatic for countrymen (Miller, 1963). Men living and working in the country tend not to lose prestige and status on retirement to the extent that city dwellers often do. They usually have many and varied skills, ample opportunities to work part-time, and the social traditions of the countryside contribute to an atmosphere in which the line between employment and retirement is more blurred than it is in urban areas.

Level of education is linked to socio-economic status, but its effect on felt loss of status in retirement has been noted in one study (Lipman, 1964). The higher the educational level, the smaller the percentage who viewed retirement as a loss of self-worth.

Finally, it should be pointed out that the influences on coping with retirement noted above – sex, class, urban-rural, education – do not exhaust the range of possible influences that have yet to be studied. For example, it is somewhat surprising that the independent influence on retirement of income level (apart from occupation and education which are obviously related to income) has not apparently been given any attention, and the same applies to type of housing and availability of public or private transport. Perhaps future research will deal with these and other possible influences on the experience of retirement.

Mortality

In any informal gathering where the consequences of retirement are discussed it is likely that someone will relate how a person –usually a man – known to them died within a short while of being retired. In the literature, too, there are some statements which appear to be unsubstantiated assertions rather than reports of proper studies, for example, 'the first year of retirement is marked by a heavy mortality rate' (Sauvy, 1948). It is particularly important, therefore, in seeking to understand the relationship between retirement and mortality to beware of conventional wisdom, whether it says that retirement has a good or a bad effect on mortality.

One source of data on this subject is insurance company mortality tables. In quoting from one of these, Hart (1957) states: 'If you retire in good health at any of the usual retirement ages, with an income adequate for your needs, you will live four or five years longer than if you'd stayed on the job!' The clear implication is: retire and live longer. But the human situations summed up in the mortality tables contain many more variables than simply working versus retirement and shorter versus longer life. Some people who go on working after normal retirement age do so because their retirement income would not be adequate for their needs – such people are likely to be in lower socioeconomic groups whose life expectancy is shorter than for the wealthier and more privileged. To be better off is correlated with having better health, with generally being better prepared for retirement, and with being more likely to be able to choose if and when to retire – a cluster of variables all of which probably contribute in some degree to longer life, though our present state of research does not enable us to be conclusive about this or to measure the relative contributions of different variables to longer life.

A significant variable in accounting for differential mortality rates before and after retirement is whether the retirement is early or 'normal'. Early retirement, as we saw earlier, is very often the result of poor health, which would lead to a greater chance of an early death. This is confirmed by research on rubber-tyre workers in the USA, which indicates that pre-retirement health is a significant predictor of survival after early retirement (Haynes, McMichael and Tyroler, 1977, 1978). Among 'normal' retirees lower-status workers were more likely to die within three years of retirement than higher-status workers, who were more prominent among deaths four to five years after retirement. The authors think this may imply a 'disenchantment' phase – if so, the higher-status workers seem to take longer to become disenchanted with retirement than the lower-status workers.

Earlier research (Myers, 1954) had suggested that 'the mortality of retired workers during the first year or two of retirement is considerably above the general level which otherwise might be expected but thereafter merges with such general level'. The higher mortality rate is attributed to the fact that those in poorer health are more apt to retire, or, as Thompson and Streib (1958) put it, 'mortality among the retired population may be artificially padded with people who choose to retire *because* of their poor health'. However, other research in Canada among pensioners in a large communications company suggests that death rates are not higher shortly after retirement (Tyhurst, Salk and Kennedy, 1957). Also, research in Finland found that retirement did not increase mortality and that it was for most people not a psycho-social stress situation that would lead to such an increase (Niemi, 1980).

In Britain, analysis of census data shows that among both men and women under state pension age the retired have death rates nearly twice as high as for the employed (Fox, 1979). Further unpublished analysis indicates that, for those over pension age, the difference is in the same direction but much less marked, no doubt because the reason for retirement after pension age is much less often ill-health. A separate check on suicide-type causes of death offered no support for the hypothesis that suicide is more prevalent among the retired than among workers, whether under or over pension age. However, in the USA persons over 65, who comprise only 9 per cent of the population, account for 25 per cent of all suicides (Hopper and Guttmacher, 1979). Those who attempt or complete suicide have been shown often to have been through personal crises or disruptive life events, and some suspicion must attach to retirement as the main or contributory cause of such crises or disruptions in at least some cases.

The general conclusion, then, on the relationship between retirement and mortality has to be an open verdict. Clearly poor health can lead to both early retirement and early death, in which case it seems fairer to attribute death to poor health rather than to retirement. By the same token, the lower death rates of workers compared with the retired should be attributed to better health rather than to being in employment.

Wives' Attitudes to Husbands' Retirement

If both husband and wife have been working, and one of them retires, it would generally seem desirable for the other to retire too, so that both can spend more time together. It is not clear how often such 'double' retirements actually happen, though there are indications that they are fairly widespread, especially if cases of retirement a few months apart are included. If the wife has remained a full-time homemaker, however, she will not retire in the usual sense of that term, though she will probably be profoundly affected by her husband's retirement. An important variable here is the husband's own attitude to his retirement: if he makes a poor adjustment she may find the unaccustomed presence of a demoralised husband around the house to be more disruptive than welcome (Rapoport, Rapoport and Strelitz, 1977).

American research on attitudes of wives to their husbands' retirement suggests that the reason for retirement and the socio-economic level of the retiree are among the more important influences on these attitudes. In their longitudinal study of thirty-three couples in North Carolina, Heyman and Jeffers (1966, 1968) report that 45 per cent of wives were glad their husbands had retired and 55 per cent were sorry. 'Sad' wives tended to be older, in poorer health, low in activities and unhappy in their marriages, and they often had manual-worker husbands who had retired early because of ill-health. In cases of retirement due to health, 72 per cent of the wives were sorry about it, but when the retirement was mandatory 64 per cent of the wives were glad.

In a later study by Fengler (1975) wives were divided into three groups according to their attitude to their husbands' retirement. The pessimists feared that their husbands would find themselves with a surplus of time on their hands or that they would intrude into the wives' domestic domain. These wives thought that the failure of their husbands to develop non-work interests would result in their domestic routine being disturbed and new demands on their time and energy. The optimistic wives looked forward to an exciting new life together with their husbands: they did not perceive retirement as a threat and welcomed the opportunity to share more activities with their husbands. The third group – neutralists – saw retirement bringing no change in their marital situation. In Fengler's sample 39 per cent were classified as optimists, 32 per cent as pessimists, and 29 per cent as neutralists.

Conclusion

Many people, especially men, retire early because of ill-health –the more fortunate minority are happy to retire early because they have reasonable occupational pensions. Ill-health, though still important, has been declining as a reason for early retirement in recent years, and 'administrative' retirement has been increasing.

Although most people adjust reasonably well to retirement, about a third have some difficulty: adjustment often means simply making the best of things. The gains of retirement – freedom, getting rid of undesired work and its consequences – are balanced by losses of valued work experiences and of the feeling of being useful. Retirement has various positive and negative meanings to those concerned, and the negative meanings seem slightly to outweigh the positive. Physical health is generally improved by retirement but this is not so for mental health. Retirement can be like sickness, divorce or bereavement in its effects, but there is uncertainty about whether it has a good or bad influence on mortality. Husbands and wives may retire either together or at varying times, and wives are glad that their husbands retire about as often as they are sorry.

6

Work after Retirement Age

There are several ways in which some form of work features in the lives of people who have passed normal retirement age. One way consists of continued work for the same employer, though sometimes with lighter tasks or shorter hours. Another possibility is a change of type of work, perhaps a second or even third career. And beyond the realm of conventional employment some form of useful work can be engaged in, such as collective barter of work products or services, or voluntary contributions to educational, welfare or community activities. In this chapter we shall first examine the types of employment engaged in by workers over normal retirement age and the various types of non-employment work. Then we shall say something about types of older workers and reasons for working, and conclude with a section on the difficulties and consequences of working after retirement age.

Employment of Older Workers

Although the average age of retirement is tending to come down in modern industrial societies, the changing age structure on a global scale means that the total number of older workers is likely to increase in the coming years. Global figures given by the International Labour Office (1979) show a total of 475 million workers aged 45+, with the number expected to rise to almost 700 million by the year 2,000. In the USA and Europe workers aged 45+ represent about 35 per cent of all workers.

According to 1971 British census figures, 88 per cent of men aged 60–64 (that is, those within five years of state pension age) were in employment, but only 31 per cent of those aged 65–69. For women the comparable groups are aged 55–59 and 60–64 and 51 and 28 per cent respectively were in employment. The proportion of men employed in the 65–69 age group has been going down steadily: in 1931 it was 65 per cent, in 1951 47 per cent and in 1971 31 per cent. This is part of an international trend: less than 15 per cent of all persons over 65 participate in the labour force in Canada, France, the Federal Republic of Germany, Italy, the Netherlands, Sweden and the USA (Morrison, 1979).

The types of work engaged in by people after normal retirement age differ in a number of ways from the types of work engaged in by younger people. There are two related reasons for this: some types of work are regarded as unsuitable for (and others as specially suitable for) older workers, and there are differences in the retirement policies of employers which differentially affect skill levels. These factors combine to produce different distributions of types of work among younger and older workers. Those over pension age average fewer weekly working hours than do workers during the ten years prior to state pension age: men average twenty-five hours as against forty-two, and women twenty-two hours as against twenty-seven (Parker, 1980).

In addition to the differences between employment opportunities for younger and older workers, there are also some similarities. Because older workers are sometimes regarded by employers as inferior substitutes for younger workers, variations in the age structure of a population may affect employment opportunities for older persons. In general, these opportunities vary inversely with the rate at which young people are added to the population of working age. When younger workers are withdrawn from the labour force, for example in wartime, employment opportunities for older workers increase.

It is sometimes assumed that the jobs of workers after normal retirement age are very similar to those of younger workers, except that heavy physical work is less frequent among the former. This assumption is at the root of the claim that it is wrong for older workers to 'hang on' in jobs which younger workers could do. But few men over pension age have skilled manual jobs – 11 per cent compared with 32 per cent under pension age – and more have unskilled manual jobs – 21 per cent compared with 5 per cent (Parker, 1980). Among women there is a similar tendency towards unskilled manual work over pension age – 22 per cent compared with 10 per cent under – and this is partly balanced by fewer junior non-manual jobs over pension age such as clerks and typists – 24 per cent compared with 32 per cent under. Also, census data from the USA suggest that better-educated people with higher incomes tend to continue to work after normal retirement age (Jaffe, 1970), a trend which is probably also true of Britain and other countries.

On the subject of employment for the retired, Clark (1973) writes, 'we can assume from the figures [of unofficial agencies] that, when a retired man gets a part-time job, there is an even chance that it will be that of a handyman or a cleaner, or perhaps a combination of the two'. This assumption is quite wrong. As noted above, four in five men workers over pension age (including a majority of part-timers) are *not* in unskilled manual jobs; furthermore, some of these latter jobs (for example, labourers, porters, guards) fall outside the categories of handyman and cleaner. According to Tinker (1981), 'the 1971 census shows that where occupations were classified retired men and women were mainly employed in service, sport and recreation'. It shows no such thing. A mere 16 per cent of men aged 65 or over were employed in these occupations, although as many as 42 per cent of women 60 or over were employed in them.

The industrial distribution of jobs held by workers over pension age is not markedly different from the industrial distribution of jobs held by younger workers (Parker, 1980). There are some differences, such as the sharp reduction of older workers in mining, but other workers are employed roughly *pro rata* in all industries grouped together in the Standard Industrial Classification. However, it does appear that some particular industries are more likely than others to allow older workers with certain skills to continue. What Clark and Dunne (1955) call 'survival rates' (based on the percentage of men capable of remaining in jobs into their late 60s or beyond) were high among makers of watches, clocks and musical instruments and low among coal-face workers and signalmen. The fact that some kinds of skilled work have been replaced in recent years by automated processes is part of the explanation of the lower proportion of the elderly now in employment.

Data from the USA suggest that the pattern of older workers' employment is similar in some ways but different in others to that in Britain. In the USA, elderly workers are less likely than others to have blue-collar jobs, but are more likely to have service or farm jobs (Manard, 1975). According to a study by Bengston, Chiribosa and Keller (1969) 'retired' schoolteachers were much more likely to be still working than retired steel-workers. In Britain there is the same overall trend away from manual jobs with increasing age, but only because the rise in unskilled jobs is outweighed by the fall in skilled jobs. In the USA elderly workers are more often either self-employed or work for small businesses or private households, as compared with younger workers (Epstein and Murray, 1968). But in Britain there is no evidence that this is the case.

American census data show that older workers are over-represented in occupations that are on the wane, stationary, or increasing only very slowly; they are under-represented in new and rapidly growing occupations that require special and newer skills (Lehman, 1955). All the indications are that this trend has continued in the USA and is also operative in Britain.

Other analysis based on American data suggests that workers over 65 tend to be drawn from the extremes of the occupational ladder, being either lower or upper occupational class (Fillenbaum and Maddox, 1974). Also, the 'working retired' have been found to differ from the non-working retired in having a longer schooling, intending to work when retired, and being less likely to report a deterioration in health (Fillenbaum, 1971*a*, 1971*b*). The 'working retired' were said to have less financial need to work and to hold membership in a larger number of associations, which may be interpreted as implying a greater involvement in work in the broad sense of activity.

The pattern of employment among older workers in Japan is somewhat different to that in the USA and Britain. Well over half the aged men in Japan continue to work (Palmore, 1975). The customary retirement age in most businesses is about 55, but this usually means simply switching to another company, to another job in the same company, or to self-employment. More than half of workers in Japan aged 55 or over are farmers, lumbermen, or fishermen.

There are also socio-economic differences in the possibilities of remaining employed after pension age. In a survey of four urban areas Abrams (1978) found that, on reaching pension age, the average professional or managerial (AB) man reduces his paid work time by less than 40 per cent, while the semi-skilled and unskilled manual (DE) group cease paid employment almost entirely. The professional man or woman can reach pension age with good health, work they like, and their own options in continuing it; the artist, too, can usually go on doing what he has always done for the joy of it.

Non-Employment work

Work in the wider sense of productive activity need not cease after paid employment or self-employment has been given up. The older individual can engage in activities, outside the sphere of employment, which reward him in some financial or non-financial way or which are aimed at rewarding others. Self-rewarding non-employment work activities consist of various forms of do-it-yourself or collective barter of work products and services; other-rewarding non-employment work activities (which may, of course, imply an important element of self-reward as a consequence or secondary motivation) include voluntary contributions to educational, welfare and community activities.

In recent years there has been a growth among most sections of the population in do-it-yourself activities. This has been mainly because of the increasing cost of labour, which makes it attractive to buy goods in a form which embodies low labour content. Factories and retail outlets have been developed which supply ready-to-assemble materials to customers willing to add their own labour to obtain a finished product. According to the *General Household Survey, 1979* (1980), 35 per cent of the adult population engaged in household repairs or do-it-yourself during the four weeks prior to interview, although the percentage declined somewhat with increasing age, no doubt mainly due to physical limitations.

Beyond do-it-yourself, the other main type of self-rewarding non-employment work activity is collective barter. The simplest and most widespread form of such barter is the informal exchange of labour between members of a family living in the same household. 'I'll wash up and you wipe' is an obvious example, but in communities of several families or individuals living together a roster is often devised to reduce the frequency of having to do such chores while increasing the number of people who are rendered a service on each occasion. Other forms of barter of labour extending beyond particular families, and involving some degree of prior organisation, are baby-sitting and car-sharing.

In recent years a further form of barter of labour has been devised which goes somewhat beyond the arrangements described above and which is designed particularly to meet the needs of retired people to work and to receive the fruits of other people's work. Link Opportunity is a self-help scheme set up a few years ago on an experimental basis in a number of local areas in Britain (Blaire, 1977; *Pre-Retirement Choice*, 1976). It provides the over 60s with the opportunity to play an active role in the community, using skills and crafts officially abandoned on retirement. Work of a particular kind is performed on an hourly basis, in exchange for a labour token which can be used to obtain the benefits of the work of others – thus, for example, an hour's gardening can be exchanged for an hour's teaching of French. The scheme enables the elderly to obtain services that otherwise they may not be able to afford, and since no money is involved, to reciprocate without worrying about income tax or earnings limits affecting their pension rights.

So far we have considered one type of non-employment work: that concerned primarily with bringing advantage to oneself. The other major type is aimed at bringing advantage to other people, although the doers of this kind of work may themselves be partly motivated by the personal acclaim it brings them and may hence derive self-satisfaction from their efforts. According to the official British survey (Parker, 1980), 17 per cent of retirees were doing some form of voluntary or unpaid work. Although no inquiry was made in that survey about the willingness of retirees to undertake voluntary or unpaid work, other evidence (Desai and Naik, 1974) suggests that probably about one in six retired people are willing to take up voluntary social work.

Older people can derive various satisfactions from voluntary or unpaid work. For many, participation in such work, and the social contacts it brings, are important in providing a reason for living. Those who live in retirement communities often find that taking voluntary 'work' roles within the community offers higher status than the more complete 'retirement' of doing nothing or participating only in social or recreational activities (Gubrium, 1974). In terms of how an individual regards himself and wishes to be regarded by others, retirement from paid work does not necessarily mean becoming a retiring person: though retired from the productive process, a person may still be active in other circles.

In recent years in the USA a number of new and imaginative programmes have been introduced by private and government agencies which offer opportunities for older citizens to engage in service roles. Examples are foster grandparents and a 'dial-a-friend' telephone service. Not all such roles are acceptable to retired people, and there is the danger that if the 'work' is seen as too trivial or meaningless it will also be seen as demeaning. But for those who are reasonably adaptable and take on the work in a willing spirit, the rewards are often great. Because voluntary and unpaid work is more often engaged in by the better-educated, there are more schemes for involving such people than the lesser-educated or those retired from unskilled jobs. Thus the Institute for Retired Professionals at the New School for Social Research in New York City offers work on campus to 'educated retirees' as teachers, leaders and administrators.

Reasons for Working

Several inquiries have thrown light on the reasons why people continue to work after normal retirement age, either in the same or a different job. These inquiries fall into two broad groups: based on older people generally and based on groups of particular kinds. In addition to these empirical inquiries, other observers have contributed insights and propositions about why some older people continue to work or need to do so.

The recent British survey (Parker, 1980) on older workers and

129

retirement asked about the main reasons for continuing to work after normal retirement age (see Table 6.1).

Table 6.1

	Men	Women
	(*in percentages*)	
Need the money	42	40
Would be bored otherwise	21	13
Like the work	17	21
Was asked to stay on by employer	3	2
Spouse not retired	1	7

It should be noted that these are only main reasons: many informants gave more than one reason, including liking the companionship of workmates and 'to keep well, active or fit'.

In a previous British national inquiry carried out in 1953 it was found that nearly half of the men who chose to stay on at work after 65 said it was a question of money, and a similar number said they preferred to work or that they felt fit enough to continue; many gave both reasons (National Advisory Committee, 1955). Because of the different research methods used in the two surveys, it is not possible to draw conclusions about any changes that might have taken place between the survey dates, but it does seem that the general picture of half financial and half non-financial reasons has remained fairly constant, with some individuals giving both reasons.

A survey in 1977 among the nine EEC countries showed that, among the 24 per cent of the population aged 15 and over who thought that they would try to get a paid job when they got their pension, about 70 per cent would do so because they wanted to stay active and 25 per cent to increase their income (Riffault, 1978). No separate figures were given for each country, though it was noted that more people in the UK than in the other countries said they would seek work.

Surveys in the USA show results similar to those in Britain. An inquiry in the Midwest among 2,000 men and women over 65 found that of those who were still working a half indicated that they did so because they liked to work and the other half because they needed the money (Hansen, Yoshioka, Taves and Caro, 1965).

Inquiries among particular sections of older workers bring out differences in motivation among those in various socio-economic, occupational and other groups. As one might expect, many workers in low socio-economic groups, who have relatively little savings, and smaller occupational pensions if any, tend to continue working or take up new work after pension age because they need the extra money. Among older workers the main reason for preferring to remain at work is that retirement would bring some form of economic hardship or at least a reduction in standards of living. A reason overlooked by most survey research, but which no doubt has its appeal for some people, is that they are looking for a legitimate excuse to spend a few hours away from home.

American research into the motivations of older and relatively deprived groups to work is not quite so conclusive about the dominance of money. Retired recipients of social security benefits have been said to be mainly interested in additional income to maintain something like the previous standard of living, rather than in being busy or useful (Stecker, 1951). But it has also been suggested that older workers of low socio-economic status frequently have an 'obsessive desire' for work in order to 'maintain self-esteem, the wish to escape from self-preoccupation and depression, and the striving to combat inner restlessness' (Fried, 1949). If this seems to be an over-rational account of why older working-class people go on working, we should remember the quiet desperation of Arthur, the ex-messenger faced with the emptiness of a life without work.

Much attention has been paid to the motivation of some older professional people to go on working. The selection of professions to be studied has not been representative of all professionals but heavily oriented to the academic world. Kratcoski, Huber and Gaulak (1974) asked ninety-three retired emeritus professors in one university what factors helped them to adjust to retirement and led to feelings of satisfaction: 40 per cent mentioned continued work activities, 18 per cent continued professional contacts, and most of the rest gave hobbies or other non-work interests. In other words, over half were still actively involved in their professional work, despite being 'retired'. Acuff and Allen (1970) found their sample of retired professors similarly engaged, and noted that such engagement seemed to be significantly related to purpose in life.

More than half of a small sample of 'retired' Chicago schoolteachers were found to be still employed (Bengston, Chiribosa and Keller, 1969): 'For most, work seemed to be pleasurable but neither an economic nor a psychic necessity. Most stressed that their post-retirement employment meant continued interaction with esteemed colleagues and a chance to be of continued service to the community . . . ' In the absence of research on the motivation of non-academic professionals to work after retirement age, one may reasonably speculate that contact with colleagues is a very popular source of satisfaction, but that the motivation of service to the community is widespread only in those professions aimed at giving such service.

A number of writers have offered interpretations of the reasons why people go on working after retirement age, apparently basing their views on personal observation and intuitive reasoning rather than on empirical inquiry. Happiness is a frequent theme of such interpretations. A typical statement, no doubt echoed by many happy working retirees, is that of Rynne (1973): 'For many people, the only way to be really happy in retirement is to go on working in some capacity or other.' Stearns (1977) sees elderly workers as one of two happy groups, the other being active hobbyists: 'The happiest older males seem to be those who can maintain some hold on the work ethic . . . or who plump for a life of hobbies, gardening, perhaps travel and a change of residence.' Anne Simon (1968), too, is against what she calls 'the idleness idea', contrasting it with the possibility of being committed to work and enjoying it. Our three activists – Norman, Meg and Jean – certainly confirm that happiness, or at least contentment, in retirement is likely to result from keeping up old interests or involvements, or developing new ones.

Demand for Work

There is no doubt that some form of paid work is wanted by a substantial proportion of people who are now retired or who have passed state pension age. Four relevant questions are: How many of the retired want work? What kind of retired people are these? What kinds of work do they want? Why do they want to work? Research findings are available to help answer all these questions.

The recent national survey of older workers and retirement showed that, in addition to 3 per cent of men and 1 per cent of women over pension age being unemployed (that is, actively seeking work), a further 10 per cent of the 'retired' men and 7 per cent of 'retired' women said there was a period after their last job ended when they were looking for paid work (Parker, 1980). No doubt many of these had given up seriously looking because the work was not available. Furthermore, 9 per cent of 'retired' men and 12 per cent of 'retired' women said that they might at some time in the future do paid work again. Most of those who said they might work again preferred part-time hours but were prepared to work all the year round.

Age Concern (1974) conducted a survey of 2,700 men and women over pension age and found that 10 per cent of the retired would like a paid job, rising to 21 per cent among newly retired men. Even at age 75 and over, 6 per cent of women and 5 per cent of men would like to have a job. Among those whose health was rated worst, 7 per cent wanted a job – not markedly lower than the 11 per cent among the healthier group. More than half of the retirees who wanted a paid job said they were not happy to retire.

In other European countries the demand among the retired for work seems even greater than in Britain. Research in the Scandinavian countries shows that over 50 per cent of retired persons want to be gainfully employed, and similar proportions are to be found in France and Switzerland (Council of Europe, 1977). According to a recent Swedish survey, 66 per cent of men and women aged 60–75 had a positive attitude to continued work, but only 40 per cent had actually worked since retirement (Skoglund, 1979). Among retired men aged 68–73 in Denmark, one quarter wish for some form of employment (Olsen and Hansen, 1977). Even among British retired movers to the seaside – who might be expected to think more in terms of a new leisure life than of continuing work – a quarter to a third would have preferred to continue working (Karn, 1974).

133

Data from the American Retirement History Study suggest that the desire of older people for work is less marked than in Europe. After eliminating about half of those aged 58–67 whose health considerably limited the kind or amount of work they could do, just under a quarter of men and just over a quarter of women were found to be available for work (Motley, 1978).

On the subject of what kind of retired people want work, it seems that a higher proportion of the recently retired do so than of those who have been retired three years or more (Shanas, 1972). Reasons for retirement also seem to be linked with a desire for re-employment, which applies especially to those dismissed without warning, having experienced illness or redundancy, all of which tend to leave the individual unprepared for retirement.

The finding quoted above that part-time work is often wanted by retirees in Britain seems also to apply in the USA. From a survey in the Midwest, Hansen and his colleagues (1965) found that 23 per cent of the fully retired wanted part-time work and 17 per cent full-time work; these proportions have probably fallen since the time of that survey, but there is no reason to suppose that there has been a drastic change in the relative proportions seeking part- and full-time work. Many people want to continue in the same kind of work, but sometimes a desired upgrading in status is mentioned, such as a labourer wanting bench work or a cleaner wanting clerical work.

Difficulties and Consequences

The biggest difficulty facing older people who want to work is the attitude of many employers, based mostly on unfounded prejudices against employing them. As we saw in Chapter 4, there are some kinds of job for which older workers are generally unsuited and it is reasonable that prospective employers are reluctant to take on older people in these capacities. However, many employers do discriminate against older workers simply because of negative stereotypes that they hold and other mistaken or irrational beliefs about older workers. Sometimes the discrimination is not open and is disguised by an apparent willingness to employ older workers. Thus Shenfield (1955) found that, while most employers expressed themselves as in no way averse to employing people over pension age, they almost invariably then went on to demonstrate that this would be impossible, however, in their particular trade.

Some observers other than employers expound the difficulties of employing older workers in a rather unsympathetic way. Take, for example, the following remarks by Szalai (1976):

> ... proposals to provide the old and retired with 'suitable' opportunities for doing productive work encounter even greater organisational, motivational and financial difficulties. In view of the reduced mobility of old people and the great variety of their individual infirmities, such opportunities of work would have to be literally hand-picked. The types of 'suitable' work which would be available in a modern indus-trialised society for such purposes are mostly left-overs from the age of handicrafts: primitive, monotonous, repetitive jobs which were always so badly paid that nobody cared to replace the labourers involved in such menial tasks by machines.

There is some truth and a lot of unfounded prejudice in Szalai's statements. Some older people do have reduced mobility but this does not prevent them from being suitable for jobs in which mobility is not at a premium; many older people are just as mobile as younger colleagues. The 'greater variety' of individual infirmities with older age is illusory: there are no diseases of old age, just diseases which tend to be more common with advancing age (and some less common). Older people do tend to be offered work at lower rates of pay, and some understandably refuse such offers, but as for 'suitable' work being primitive, monotonous and repetitive, these are the characteristics of much work offered to young people, and highly skilled handicraft work is often found to be very suitable indeed to the talents and abilities of older people.

The objections put up by employers to having older workers on their payroll are too often echoed in the defeatist attitude of many older job seekers. To be unemployed and saddled with a defeatist attitude creates fear and insecurity instead of hope and confidence. Many older people have forgotten how to sell themselves to a prospective employer or misguidedly feel that they are too old to learn new skills. Too often the model is accepted of older workers slowing down to the point of exhaustion, and hence being entitled to rest during their last days. This model corresponds to that of people as adjuncts to machines, which wear out or become obsolescent. But many older workers and potential workers are healthy and vigorous, not exhausted or obsolescent.

Once older people have overcome the difficulties facing them in retaining or obtaining paid work, the consequences seem, on the whole, to be very favourable to them. The provision of part-time work for retired people seems especially to have been markedly successful for all concerned. Research has shown a positive relation between the activity of older people and their general satisfaction with life. Whether the work is paid or unpaid does not seem to be a vital factor in producing beneficial results: those inmates of a home for the aged who assumed work tasks in the home scored higher on adjustment attitude scales than did non-workers (Kleemeier, 1951).

Work does seem to have a rejuvenating effect on at least some older men and women. Work satisfaction has been found to be positively correlated with longevity (Palmore, 1969; C. L. Rose, 1964). Most people who live a long time continue to work at something throughout their lives. A New York study showed that only 18 per cent of employed people in their 60s said that they were old, whereas 37 per cent of retirees of the same age did (R. Jones, 1977). Leaving life on a high note of activity is well expressed by the remark of one informant in another survey: 'I'd rather work out than rust out.'

Conclusion

Although most men and women stop work at state pension age, a sizeable minority continue to be employed, mostly part-time. Apart from heavy manual work such as mining, the jobs that older workers have are generally not different from those of younger workers. Older people can and do engage in non-employment work such as do-it-yourself, collective barter and voluntary work. About half of the older workers are employed because they need the money, but others have non-financial reasons such as liking the work or avoiding boredom. Most of the retirees who want work prefer part-time hours, but they face age-prejudiced employers and too often have a socially induced defeatist attitude to getting work.

The stress on employment rather than on other forms of work leaves the elderly at a disadvantage in our society – it is part of an approach which seeks to separate productive and 'engaged' younger people from non-productive and 'disengaged' older people. But since work has a rejuvenating effect on at least some older men and women, and since their contribution to the wealth and welfare of the community can be valuable, it is an unjustifiably restrictive policy to deny work opportunities to those who need them.

7
Retirement as Leisure?

What are the similarities and differences between the concepts of retirement and leisure? How far do work-leisure relationships and preparation for retirement influence the experience of retirement? There are positive and negative views about how far people do experience retirement as leisure. With these questions and different general approaches in mind, we may look at the ways in which older and retired people tend to spend their free time. The chapter concludes with an assessment of new attitudes to leisure and of meanings sought and found in leisure activities during the period of retirement.

Concepts of Retirement and Leisure

In everyday parlance the state of retirement is frequently associated with the state of being at leisure. If leisure is defined residually as the absence of work then the temptation to make the association is increased, for retirement is also the absence of work. The credibility of the association is further increased by thinking of both retirement and leisure in terms of time rather than quality of activity or experience: leisure is something for which we have time at the end of the working day, week, year — and of the working life. Moreover, there is in the conventional wisdom about work, retirement and leisure a means/end or effort/reward connection: after a lifetime of work, a person is thought to be entitled to a few years of well-earned leisure. That is the central myth of retirement, although the myth itself is ambiguous because people's relation to their work takes various forms. If work is an unpleasant means to earning a living, then the leisure of retirement is compensation for effort expended and time wasted. But if work is a positive experience then the leisure of retirement is not compensation but a replacement for something valued which has been lost.

Whether work is experienced as positive or negative, pleasant or unpleasant, as an end in itself or only as a means to an end, anticipated leisure is at the core of the myth of retirement. It is appropriate to regard it as a myth because it is not the reality which many people experience in retirement. There is often an unrealistic expectation that the role of leisure will increase in retirement, and an unjustified belief that leisure can offer adequate compensation or reward for the loss of work.

The notion that retirement can compensate for or replace work involves the belief that the role of leisure in the life of the individual will increase or change with the advent of retirement. The role of leisure in retirement has been the subject of a number of studies in recent years. In general, the findings emphasise continuity of lifestyle from the pre-retirement to the retirement period. Thus Atchley (1971*b*) writes about a lifestyle developed in middle age which is retained as much as possible into old age, not so much in terms of simply maintaining activity levels but in terms of preserving a continuity of psychological commitment to a particular lifestyle.

Ageing has a rather insignificant influence on people's recreational patterns and preferences. There may be a necessity to give up or curtail certain activities due to social pressures, but the general tendency is in the direction of retaining the patterns of living which have been developed in the past. One study showed a general decrease in leisure activity participation from age 16 to 69, but the selection of leisure activities was not altered to any degree in the same age range (Cunningham, Montoye, Metzner and Keller, 1968).

Research evidence suggests that the ageing process does not normally bring about a fundamental change in the type or quality of leisure behaviour. There *are* differences between the ways in which retired and non-retired persons experience leisure, and we shall consider some of these below. But there is no reason to suppose that 'retirement' leisure represents a dramatically new set of behaviours in more than a minority of cases. As Peppers (1976) puts it, 'contrary to the popular notion that retirement brings with it a prescribed group of "acceptable" leisure pursuits, the subjects involved in this research were engaged in a wide range of activities, from gambling to reading, horse-breeding to bird-watching, golf to team sports. Perhaps the only general statement that can be made concerning the nature of leisure activity in retirement is that there is no specific retirement activity.'

Work/Leisure Relationships, Retirement Preparation and Experience

Does what we call leisure in earlier working life retain its same significance when not integrated into the work cycle? Two of the most important influences on the quality of life and leisure in retirement (among others, no doubt) are the extent of preparation for retirement and the previous relationship between work and leisure in the life of the individual. In Chapter 3 we considered the various measures which have been taken to prepare people for retirement. For the present purpose we shall posit a simple dichotomy of individuals as prepared or not prepared for retirement. The second influence on retirement to be examined is that of the relationship during the main part of working life between work and leisure. Here there is very little research and consequent literature to guide us. I propose, therefore, to rely on using a sociological imagination to extend into the normal retirement period my own research-based hypotheses concerning the work/leisure relationship.

The three types of work/leisure relationship which I have identified are extension, opposition and neutrality (Parker, 1972). Briefly, the extension pattern consists in having leisure activities which are often similar in content to one's work and of making no sharp distinction between what is considered as work and what as leisure. With the opposition pattern leisure activities are deliberately unlike work and there is a sharp distinction between what is work and what is leisure. Thirdly, the neutrality pattern is, in some respect, intermediate between the first two but differs from them in being characterised by detachment from active involvement in either work or leisure.

How are people with these three patterns of work/leisure

relationship, each either prepared or unprepared for retirement, likely to anticipate and adjust to a life of so-called leisure in retirement?

Let is first take the case of a person with the extension pattern, which would typically mean a life centred around work, albeit work consisting of a varied and deeply satisfying set of experiences. Leisure for that kind of person would probably be a poorly developed area of life, partly because working life is so rich. Faced with the prospect of retirement, the 'extension' person can prepare himself or herself for the consequent change – or can choose (as a minority undoubtedly does) to reject it as a possible way of life. Rejection is a tenable stance if there is a choice about whether to retire to go on working, but it is the worst possible stance if retirement at a certain age is compulsory and no alternative work is available.

The 'extension' person who is prepared for retirement probably has sufficient resources, developed in the work sphere, to carry him or her over successfully and happily into a retirement of active leisure – retirement will be seen as a new adventure. Norman, our ex-sales manager, certainly had this attitude to his active new life in retirement, although he was not 'prepared' for retirement in the sense of having thought long about it and attended courses on it. But the 'extension' man or woman who, because of rejecting the idea of retirement, is unprepared to experience it is likely to find it very difficult to make an adequate adjustment. This is the kind of person who often feels 'lost', at least in the early period of retirement, though a reasonably flexible outlook and some opportunities for meaningful activities will help the process of subsequent adjustment.

The 'opposition' person faces retirement in an entirely different way. Since work is a hated experience (or is at least regarded with a mixture of love and hate) the loss of it will be relished. But once again preparation is a key variable. The 'opposition' person who is prepared for retirement must thereby be prepared for a very big change in attitude to daily activities. The person whose hatred of work is unmixed with more positive feelings may well have a predominantly negative outlook on life, and so may come to hate retirement as much as work.

Successful preparation for retirement would mean the

141

transfer of any 'love' element in work to some appropriate non-work activity, with a reduction of the 'hate' element as a result of the constraints of work being removed. The 'opposition' person unprepared for retirement will tend to miss the tension between the work and the leisure parts of life – the former black and white of work and leisure may merge into a grey area of unexciting retirement. Also, leisure will lose its recuperative, compensatory function in relation to work, and may not easily gain another function.

It is tempting to suppose that the 'neutrality' person will make the best adjustment of all to retirement. It will simply mean that the leisure segment of his or her life (which is lived more or less independently from work) will expand and the work segment will have disappeared. But this is probably an over-simplistic view. The effect of preparation for retirement on this type of individual will be chiefly to enable some kind of revised structure to be imposed on daily activities when employment ceases. Failure to prepare for retirement often manifests itself for the 'neutrality' person as a failure to cope with a loss of accepted routine. The biggest danger here is that the boredom previously felt in his or her job (when leisure was the 'being entertained' part of life) will be extended into the whole of retired life.

Perhaps I can sum up the gist of what I am hypothesising about the effect of work/leisure relationships and preparation on attitudes to and experience of retirement in the form of a diagram (see Figure 7.1).

Work / leisure Preparation	Extension	Opposition	Neutrality
Yes	A new adventure	Big adjustment to be made	Likely to work out well
No	Feel everything lost	Will miss the tension	Danger of boredom

Figure 7.1

Retirement as Leisure?

Positive and Negative Views

There is a persistent but ill-founded belief that the coming of retirement can bring a new dawn to the life pattern of the ageing individual. Optimistic statements about the enhanced role of leisure in retirement abound in the literature. For example, Friedmann (1958) refers to the years of retirement as the 'years in which man can live without the iron necessity of work. These are years of leisure.' Hochschild (1973) makes the rather dramatic assertion that 'the old are the forerunners of a future leisured society' but at least he acknowledges that 'this position wins them no status in today's society, which clearly values work most highly'.

Many such statements linking retirement with the positive experience of leisure are derived from research on the circumstances and attitudes of the relatively prosperous retired in middle-class USA. The picture does not hold for the elderly in many other industrial countries and among the poorer classes in the USA. What might be called the pessimistic view of retired persons' experience of leisure is well put by Simone de Beauvoir (1972): 'Leisure does not open up new possibilities for the retired man; just when he is at last set free from compulsion and restraint, the means of making use of his liberty are taken from him. He is condemned to stagnate in boredom and loneliness, a mere throw-out.' This view of retirement as a frustrating disappointment to those who looked forward to it is echoed by Samson (1972): 'There are so many people pathetically bored after a short while in retirement, so hopelessly at a loss to find contentment in the leisure for which they have worked so long, anticipated so eagerly.'

What are we to make of these widely differing assessments of the experience of leisure in retirement? No doubt there are extremes: some individuals make the transition from working life to retirement in an easy, well-prepared and entirely happy manner, while others suffer greatly from the change, are ill prepared for it and bitterly regret that it has to happen to them. But it seems reasonable to suppose that the majority of people fall somewhere between these two extremes. The interesting question for research is what are the factors which result in people being at different points between the extremes, and the

143

important question for policy is how to make it possible for more people to be closer to the desirable extreme than the undesirable.

Leisure activities in Retirement

If we define leisure as the time left over after work, household, personal maintenance and other similar functions have been met, then we might reasonably assume that retired people do more things in the greater amount of 'free' time they have than do workers in the same age group. But when we come to look at comparative activities of the retired and the non-retired this does not seem to be the case. According to Emerson (1959) the first year of retirement is generally characterised by passivity rather than by taking up extra hobbies or increased social participation. The norm of retired behaviour seems to be to do a little more gardening, somewhat more helping in the home, occasional shopping – and a lot more passive leisure. None of the people studied took up a new hobby.

Research in different countries confirms the essentially passive and home-based nature of retirement among the elderly. Cowgill and Baulch (1962) report that in the USA over half of the activities of senior citizens were individual leisure pursuits, slightly more than a third were with family members, 10 per cent with friends, but less than 2 per cent were in formal groups. Most of these people spent their leisure time at home, while very few made use of community, church or commercial facilities available for leisure activities. In Britain the picture is similar. Comparing the life of the retiree with that of the older worker, we are aware of how little extra seems to be put in the place of work (Harris and Parker, 1973). Though retired men are free to go out and about in the daytime, housebound activities claim twice as much of their interests as outside ones. However, men in the pre-retirement group, though going out daily to work, take a higher proportion of their pleasures outside the home. Similarly, in the Netherlands, retired people tend to find compensations for the loss of work by spending time in the home with their spouses rather than on activities outside the home (Kooy, Van't Klooster and Van Wingerden, 1968).

The extent of social integration in neighbourhood and local community is little affected by retirement. Among the middle-class men and women studied by Rosow (1967) retirement apparently did not strengthen local ties and they did not become more socially involved where they lived. Organisation membership generally declines both with age and the onset of retirement. In the Midwest it was found that the proportion of the elderly who reduced their participation in organisations was two to three times greater than the proportion becoming more active, and that the likelihood of membership in any organisation was inversely related to age (Hansen, Yoshioka, Taves and Caro, 1965).

In the recent British national survey two measures of leisure activity by older workers and the retired were used (Parker, 1980). Although half of the retirees who were doing some kind of voluntary or unpaid work said they had started it after they had retired, the proportions of older workers and the retired who were doing such work were the same (one in six). By giving people more time, retirement may help some to take up or do more of this kind of work, but it seems only to raise the level of activity of the retired group as a whole to that of their working colleagues in the same age group.

The other measure of leisure activity was active membership of clubs, associations and organisations. Among older workers 29 per cent belonged to at least one such body, compared with 32 per cent of the retired – hardly a significant difference, and membership of clubs and other bodies may not be a good indicator of active leisure in retirement.

New Attitudes to Leisure

The ways in which people approaching retirement view the role of leisure in the rest of their lives depend on a combination of prevailing social attitudes to leisure and the pattern of life which they have worked out for themselves. If the social attitudes to leisure are in a state of flux – as indeed they are in modern industrial societies – then what is selected by the individual from the range of possible attitudes may well be ones imbibed from child-

145

hood rather than those having gained more recent currency. People who have already retired will mostly have been brought up in a social atmosphere in which the values and judgements of the Protestant work ethic prevailed. Consequently, they will tend to measure self-worth, and the degree of respect to be accorded to others, largely in terms of doing paid work which gives them a social identity. Furthermore, they will usually view leisure as the reward for work, and as conditional upon work, so that leisure without work may well induce conscious or unconscious feelings of guilt. Future generations of retirees are likely to have become more accustomed to leisure in its own right rather than as a reward for work, so they will probably have less difficulty in adjusting to leisure in retirement.

Retirement comes fairly easily to those who have developed a satisfying leisure life alongside their work activities, although the character and meaning of leisure may change if its relationship with work is lost. Even for those with plenty of hobbies or interests, the change is usually more than just a quantitative expansion of time for leisure. Part of the satisfaction of leisure consists in contrasting it with work which, although it may not be consciously satisfying, is bound up with deep feelings of identity and meaning. When an individual retires he must come to see that what he formerly considered peripheral activities are not only satisfying but also significant. These leisure activities have, in short, to substitute for the meaning attached to work.

When retirement consists of withdrawal from a particular job, but not from the kind of work done in that job, there is also a new attitude to leisure. Retirement in such cases means that what used to be 'work' is now analogous to the 'hobby'. Those who are in this fortunate position include academics who give up their formal teaching and other commitments but who can continue to make a contribution to academic life in various other ways. Some hobbies which start out as spare-time activities can develop meanings to the individual which are large enough to fill what would otherwise be a void in retirement. Thus Christ (1965) describes the ways in which the stamp collector who retires from his job can expand the size and economic meaning of stamp collecting so that what was a part-time hobby becomes a full-time set of activities and interests. Another possibility is that a

146

leisure interest which involves marketable skills or experience can lead to further employment using those skills or that expertise when retirement from a job is mandatory.

The role of the retirement community in developing leisure occupations is worth considering. Opinion varies on how far old age clubs, retirement villages and suchlike actively contribute to a worthwhile leisure in retirement. It is sometimes maintained that the retirement community both capitalises upon, and legitimises, new attitudes to leisure and that, with its greater opportunities for friendship interaction growing out of age-grading, it functions as 'a supportive reference group for leisure-oriented life styles' (Wood and Bultena, 1969). On the other hand, retirement communities may be criticised as merely providing passive entertainment for people to pass the time and as failing to emphasise the need for personal achievement. In visiting such places one is struck by the narrow range of activities usually provided by the organisers. Leisure activities such as crafts and discussion groups often recruit only small proportions of residents, while the still-rare sheltered workshop usually has a long waiting list (Lawton, 1978). The workshop is more consistent with earlier work-oriented lifestyles.

The questions of whether retirees feel that they have a life of leisure, whether they like or dislike this, and what activities they would welcome the opportunity of engaging in, are insufficiently researched. However, it is clear that individual preferences vary substantially, as do individual feelings about being at leisure. In one study of free-time activities of aged persons, 41 per cent said they had only a few hours free each day, 39 per cent said they had all day free, and 20 per cent about half a day (Hoar, 1961). Obviously some respondents were making light of obligations to self or others which could eat into their 'free' time, while others were probably expanding these obligations because of a psychological need to minimise 'free' time.

To have leisure as part of alternating pattern of work and non-work is one thing – to have 'leisure' all the time is likely to be quite another. The leisure activities of an employed person are usually accompanied by the knowledge that he will soon have to terminate them and return to his occupational commitments. By contrast, the expectations and interpretations of leisure for the

147

retiree are non-structured and vague – he is in the position of having practically unlimited free time. Because leisure usually means something more than just free time, it would be a mistake to assume that because a person has a (retired) life of all or nearly all free time he therefore has a life of all, or nearly all, leisure.

We know too little about what freedom actually means to older people (or to younger people, for that matter) – whether it signifies choice or a kind of vacuum, and whether the alternative to freedom is negative constraint or positive commitment. One is tempted to agree with Kahn (1975) that 'retirement is wasted on the old – if they have not already learned the value of leisure' – provided that 'leisure' is interpreted broadly to mean time in which we feel free to do as we wish, including work of our own choice.

Conclusion

Although retirement is often supposed to be a period of leisure, few people appear to make a drastic change in their pattern of leisure when they retire. How they adapt to retirement is markedly influenced by how well they are prepared for it and by their previous type of work/leisure relationship. The person who has integrated his work and leisure in earlier life is likely to have developed resources to cope with retirement well, provided he has not rejected the idea of it. But the person who has kept his work and leisure separate – probably because he was bored with his job – may find it hard to cope with the loss of routine which retirement brings.

Most people who retire are fairly passive in their ways of spending time, mainly because this is a continuation of a basically passive pattern of earlier life, whether in work or leisure. Because our society still places a high moral value on work as a source of respect and identity, the 'leisure' of retirement is too often spoilt by feelings of guilt. The separation of work from leisure is essentially restrictive in its consequences for retirement: in equating retirement with leisure as the opposite of work, it cuts people off from an important source of interest, identity and fulfilment. The integration of work and leisure is expansive for retirement: in maintaining that retirement is the end of employment but not of work, it affords fresh opportunities for human expression which cut across the artificial barrier between work and leisure.

8

Policy Alternatives

In this final chapter we turn to the very important question of what choices we have in influencing the extent, experience and consequences of retirement in the future. We shall be concerned with the pros and cons of compulsory versus voluntary retirement, with the forms which flexible or gradual retirement and flexible lifestyles can take, with the provision of work for those older people who need it, with the role of education in later life, with policies for leisure, and finally with the large and speculative question of the future of retirement.

Compulsory or Voluntary Retirement?

Very few people like the idea of compulsory retirement. Many are content that the decision of their employer to retire them more or less coincides with their own wish in the matter, but others bitterly resent being, as they see it, thrown on the scrap heap. Let us look more closely at research findings which bear on attitudes to compulsory or voluntary retirement.

Jacobson's (1974*b*) investigation among industrial workers in their 50s showed that no more than 16 per cent of the women and 18 per cent of the men agreed with the statement that 'all should be retired at the same age'. According to a report in *Help Age International* (1977) an opinion poll commissioned by the National Council on Aging found that 86 per cent of the US population opposed enforced retirement on the basis of age alone. Quoting the results of an earlier survey by the same organisation, Meier (1975) concludes that 'most Americans are against forced retirement for anyone who wants to work and is able to work'. A slightly different question was posed in the Cornell survey carried out in 1951: 'Who do you think should make the decision as to when a person should retire?' Sixty per cent thought it should be 'self', 29 per cent the doctor, and 15 per cent the employer (combinations of answers were allowed). The older respondents, being closer to the decision, more often favoured 'self' making it (Barron, 1961).

There is no doubt that most people would prefer to decide for themselves if and when they should retire. Moreover, a majority also favour a retirement policy which gives other people that same right. Against this, it may reasonably be contended that people's own preferences are a poor basis for social policy as most of us, left to ourselves, would not wish to get up and go to work, pay taxes, and so on. We need, therefore, to examine in detail the reasons why policies of compulsory or of voluntary retirement should be favoured. In putting together the following lists of pros and cons I have drawn upon points made by Slavick *et al.* (1962), Palmore (1972) and Walker and Lazer (1978), among others. First the various points in favour of fixed-age retirement:

(1) *Equal treatment.* A fixed retirement age protects employees against unequal treatment by avoiding the pitfalls of judging retirement according to individual merit or circumstances. As Ginzberg (1979) puts it, no one needs to be singled out; the calendar does the dirty work.

(2) *Reduced working capacity.* Older people are less well suited to some jobs because of declining physical and mental abilities, increasing inflexibility and poorer education. A person cannot always make a sound judgement about his own declining abilities (hence the proposal that retirement should be the doctor's decision).

(3) *Saving face.* Fixed retirement saves face for the older worker with failing strength and abilities who would otherwise be singled out for forced retirement.

(4) *Making way for others.* Older workers retiring on pension can make jobs available for younger, unemployed workers; it also allows others to advance to more responsible posts.

(5) *Revitalising the employing organisation.* If older workers have to make way for younger colleagues this allows the

infusion of new ideas. A fixed retirement age has, as its basic purpose, the maintenance of a vital, dynamic and effective organisation.

(6) *Costs to employers.* It is more costly for employers to retain older workers in terms of maintaining their pensions and salaries and of their poorer health.

(7) *Planning ahead.* A compulsory retirement policy reduces uncertainty about timing and therefore encourages the employee to plan ahead for his retirement.

(8) *The legal 'average person'.* Many laws, such as those relating to achieving the age of majority, eligibility for competitive examinations, conscription, and so on, are based on the concept of the 'average person'. To leave retirement age to individual circumstances would be no more realistic than to base an individual's coming of age on his height, weight and mental development.

(9) *Difficulties of voluntary policies.* There would be great and perhaps insuperable difficulties in administering selective retirement on an individual basis. These difficulties include the devising of criteria for retirement based on abilities or performance and the circumstances in which individual preference may need to be overruled.

(10) *For the individual good.* Workers are less insecure and anxious when they know in advance the date and conditions of their retirement. Research suggests that most people make a reasonably good adjustment to retirement, even if they do not initially welcome it, and sometimes they come to wish they had been able to retire earlier.

(11) *For the collective good.* Trade unions' statements of bargaining policy place increasing emphasis on the merits of retirement and on the right of older workers to enjoy some years of leisure after long service in industry.

The arguments in favour of voluntary retirement are to some extent rebuttals of the above points but also introduce some different considerations:

(1) *Equal employment opportunity.* A fixed retirement age is contrary to the policy of equal employment opportunities

152

within broad limits of age (at least until 70). It denies individuals equal protection of the law in this regard.

(2) *Capacities not age.* Chronological age does not take into account differing abilities and capacities among older people. Many can continue to work effectively beyond 65.

(3) *Better for mental health.* Compulsory retirement leads for some to frustration and impaired mental well-being if they are capable of working adequately, want to do so, and are denied the opportunity.

(4) *Maintaining income.* Compulsory retirement can cause great economic hardship for those whose retirement income is only a fraction of their previous earnings.

(5) *Retaining skills and experience.* If skilled and experienced older people are forced to retire, the employing organisation loses the benefit of those skills and experience, and this loss is reflected at the level of national output.

(6) *Fewer social security payments.* Additional numbers of retirees cause an increase in the level of government expenditure on income-maintenance programmes and pension schemes; the declining birthrate will force a smaller labour force to support a larger retired population.

(7) *Research can help.* The problems of substituting other criteria for deciding retirement than chronological age are not insuperable. Besides the individual's own expressed wish in the matter, research may be undertaken to discover objective criteria of ageing which would be fairer and more acceptable than chronological age.

(8) *Catering for different needs.* Although retirement can be an escape into a fuller life for some, it is a dreadful, traumatic amputation for others. At whatever age compulsory retirement is fixed, the prospect casts a long shadow before it, which for some can be almost as painful as knowing when they are going to die.

(9) *Difficult transition to idleness.* The forced retirement idea is based on the belief that a man who has been taught all his life that he must be socially useful through work can make a sudden transition to idleness and still retain his self-respect.

(10) *For the individual good.* The system of compulsory retirement and inadequate pensions is a combination of contradictions. It forces some individuals to work for financial reasons who would prefer to retire, and others to retire who would prefer to continue working.

(11) *For the collective good.* One of the great wasted resources today is the talents of our senior citizens. Fortunately, talented individuals in the arts, sciences and political life are not compulsorily retired; if this principle were extended to other occupations, society would be the richer.

There is no easy way of deciding on the merits of the above arguments for and against compulsory retirement. Voluntary retirement, or at least retirement based on criteria other than chronological age, is clearly preferred by the majority of people. It may, then, be a matter of meeting the objections to voluntarism put forward by the advocates of compulsory retirement and of surmounting the difficulties of voluntarism.

In opting for the voluntary principle, it may be that many people have not fully considered the objections to it. For example, have they considered how they would feel if they were singled out by 'objective' criteria for retirement when their workmates were allowed to continue, or how much loss they would feel if they did not know at precisely what age they would be retired? My own view is that these objections are outweighed by the advantages to the individual of being given the maximum possible choice about whether and when to retire.

The arguments about older workers making way for younger and thus re-vitalising the employing organisation are more serious. It is entirely reasonable that no person past normal pension age should wilfully hang on to a position of seniority or power against the wishes and interests of those who would fill that vacated position under a policy of compulsory retirement. But all that is required is compulsory retirement from such a position when it can be demonstrated that others in the organisation are being disadvantaged. There are, however, many cases of compulsory retirement which are based on rules of thumb rather than on preventing the disadvantage of others.

Thus the forcible retirement of a skilled craftsman is not likely to disadvantage anyone, and his valuable contribution to output, including teaching others, is lost if he is forced to retire.

It is not possible to tell what proportion of the working population are, at present, subject to compulsory retirement policies. Some indication, however, is available from the recent British national survey: just over half of the men workers and a third of the women workers over pension age said they would have to give up their present job when they reached a certain age (Parker, 1980). These are substantially higher proportions than those (according to other surveys) who favour compulsory retirement and, of course, they do not include the workers who have been forced to retire before or at state pension age. Even if employers who now have compulsory retirement policies can convincingly show that completely voluntary retirement would be unworkable in their organisation, there is, nevertheless, a strong case for some degree of compromise. One form of compromise has in fact been instituted by the US government: from 1 January 1979 it has been illegal to force retirement or otherwise discriminate in employment among individuals under 70. The legislation has been described as a pragmatic compromise between the principle of functional rather than age criteria for determining who should retire and administrative or managerial convenience in retaining mandatory retirement (Sheppard, 1978). No doubt there are ways in which unscrupulous employers can circumvent such legislation, but its existence is an encouraging, if small, step in the direction of voluntarism and one which might well be adopted to good effect in other countries.

One of the biggest barriers to advancing the voluntary principle is the conservative and even capitulating attitude of some researchers and of the occasional employee who expresses a point of view. Thus Johnson (1951), after critically examining six alternatives to a compulsory retirement age (which we shall consider below under 'flexible retirement') concludes 'a compulsory retirement age is the least objectionable of the available methods, and we will therefore recommend it *even though we know of its patent weaknesses*' (emphasis mine).

The comments of another writer, Dunbar (1976), deserve reproducing and answering in full:

The most balanced, responsible and rational men and women often react in this irrational way when retirement comes and they still feel capable of doing a full day's work. They know that retirement is bound to come but when it actually does they feel a kind of terrible resentment because they weren't invited to stay on as a special case. This was admitted to me time and time again by both men and women. They felt that life had ended for everything that mattered.

The insensitivity of these remarks is almost beyond belief. Time and time again (to quote the author's own words) she was being told that compulsory retirement was unwanted, unfair and unjustified, yet she still insists that the reaction is 'irrational'. It most certainly is not irrational. It is the entirely reasonable reaction of people who can see no good reason why something they value, that is, their job, should be taken away from them just because they have reached a certain age. Although we may feel that people ought to have developed personal resources and interests to sustain them in retirement, it is no consolation to tell those who have devoted themselves to a lifetime of work that to object to giving it up is 'irrational'.

A few forcibly retired individuals do no good to the cause of voluntarism by appearing to abase themselves before the principle of what is allegedly good for 'the nation'. Thus an early retired contributor to the hopefully named *Pre-Retirement Choice* wrote: 'I suppose for the good of the nation as a whole we as individuals must be prepared to bend with the economic wind but it won't be done without a fundamental change in our thinking and the acceptance of ourselves as "tools" to be passed from hand to hand rather than individuals whose careers are sacrosanct' (Adams, 1980). In a society which pays at least lip service to the importance of the individual and to circumscribing the powers of the state, it is difficult to see what motivates the taking of such an abjectly pusillanimous position on the issue of retirement. To treat anyone as a tool diminishes his human stature. To invite others to treat oneself as a tool, and to present this as a laudable example for others to follow, is not only to hinder the progress of voluntary retirement but also to leave the door open for other and even more inhuman forms of conforming compulsion.

Flexible Retirement

The main purpose of the previous section was to discuss the pros and cons of forcing people to retire at a fixed age. Flexible retirement – using criteria other than chronological age to decide when individuals retire – contrasts with fixed retirement, and so this section is really a continuation of the previous controversy but in the form of setting out in greater detail the case for flexibility. The concept, however, is still essentially one of retirement as an event. The possibility of transforming the event into a process – gradual retirement – will be dealt with in the next section.

A number of surveys are unanimous about the working population's preference for flexible retirement, and differ only in the extent of the majorities they find in favour of it. Jacobson's (1971) study of industrial workers showed 'a predominant feeling that retirement age and rules should be more flexible and adapted to individual needs'. Among the managers and foremen surveyed by Heron and Chown (1963), 'the great majority of those interviewed preferred the idea of a flexible retirement age, and their reasons were usually based on the undoubted fact that workers of any given chronological age vary enormously in their capabilities, health and attitude to work'.

The idea of making the age of retirement much more flexible than it is at present received wholehearted support from almost all of the 8,000 people who took part in discussion groups organised by Age Concern between 1972 and 1974 (Barr, n.d.). Flexibility, it was agreed, should be the guiding principle in all matters relating to retirement, simply because of the infinite variety of individual needs and desires. Some 66 per cent of Germans questioned in a survey during the early 1970s said that they were in favour of a flexible age limit for retirement (OECD, 1973).

In the USA, Havighurst and Albrecht (1953) found that, while the attitudes of older people regarding arbitrary retirement ages are mixed, 'the majority are certainly against the idea'. A survey of 1,700 elderly citizens in Minnesota showed that a small majority of the respondents (53 per cent) objected to establishing a mandatory retirement age, and 54 per cent agreed that a flexible retirement age policy should be established (Taves and Hansen, 1963). More recently, *Nation's Business* asked its readers whether retirement should be mandatory at a certain age and four out of five said 'no' (Sheppard and Rix, 1977). Finally, in an inquiry in the Portland area, a majority of up to 90 per cent of employees, retirees, union members and non-members, personnel managers and others representing employers all rejected mandatory retirement (Weiss, 1978).

The implementation of a policy of flexible retirement requires that one or more criteria, other than a fixed age for everyone, be used to determine retirement. The following criteria are at present used to some extent, have been advocated, or are theoretically possible:

(1) *Self to decide.* This is the simplest criterion of all. It works best – some would say it only works at all – when the individual correctly assesses his own ability to carry on working or retire. It can create problems for the older worker who disregards his own poor state of health and insists on continuing work, or for his employing organisation if he stubbornly clings to a position in which he is not performing adequately. A further possible objection that the employer cannot plan ahead can be met by the worker having to give, say, six months' notice of retirement.

(2) *Market mechanisms to decide.* This criterion emphasises the relative usefulness of some older workers who should be induced to remain and the relatively poor productivity of other older workers who should be induced to retire, at least from the job in question (and being offered a more suitable job). The more highly skilled and dedicated workers could be held in the labour force by job opportunities, while lower-skilled and less-interested workers are moved to retirement. This should work reasonably well and fairly provided that judgements about skill, dedication, and so on are soundly based and preferably accepted by the worker himself. It could be tough on unskilled workers keen to work in order to supplement their pension, but no tougher in this respect than fixed-age retirement policies.

158

(3) *Job characteristics to decide.* This emphasises the varying physical or mental demands of different jobs, and it assumes that some jobs are less suitable for older workers than others. This is already recognised in the earlier retirement ages often recommended and sometimes granted in heavy industry and other physically demanding jobs. It is also a useful recognition that some jobs are well within the power of older workers, but it can be just as rigid as fixed-age retirement if it amounts to fixed-job-description retirement. The job characteristics need to be related to the workers' abilities if they are to decide retirement in a truly flexible manner.

(4) *Physical/mental fitness to decide.* In theory, this could be a variant of the 'self' criterion above (the person himself decides that he is fit or not to carry on) but most advocates suggest that a doctor makes the decision on the basis of a medical examination. This seems fair, and in fact it is often done now insofar as a doctor forbids a person in poor health to continue work. There may be difficulties, however, in marginal cases where the doctor's decision conflicts with the individuals own assessment or preference. A second opinion may help to resolve such cases satisfactorily.

Flexibility is at root about choice, and seeks circumstances and desires with opportunities. For some, the present 'normal' retirement ages may be too high; for reasons of health, liability to tiredness, difficulty of adaptation to changed methods or environment, they may wish to stop work sooner. They may also wish to stop as a matter of choice, to spend their remaining years as leisure in retirement. Others may feel themselves fit to carry on working and wish to do so. Employers who stand to lose by granting earlier occupational pensions to the first category may gain by postponing the retirement of the second category. If individual choice is valued above administrative convenience, then no one and no set of rules should force a man or woman to continue to work or to give it up against his or her wish.

Gradual Retirement

Gradual retirement should be distinguished from flexible retirement but often is not. Flexible retirement means giving up work but not at a fixed age; gradual retirement is the process of changing by at least one intermediate stage from full-time work to no work at all. Synonyms sometimes used for 'gradual' are 'phased' and 'partial'.

Unlike flexible retirement, gradual retirement has not been the subject of many surveys asking what people think about the idea. A survey of attitudes and company practice in Britain revealed that gradual or phased retirement is very popular among managers: about 80 per cent would like to be able to retire gradually but in only 7 per cent of cases is there any scheme for reducing the hours of work as the retirement date approaches (Smith, 1974).

The recent British national survey asked older people whether they preferred to retire completely at a certain age or to retire gradually, such as by working fewer hours or days and in a few years reducing to none at all (Parker, 1980). Among workers, the majority for gradual retirement was about two to one, and among retirees it was smaller but still significant. Some of the people over pension age in part-time jobs had been able to practise gradual retirement, but clearly many others had not. In a study which included interviews with 122 retired American men and women aged 50 or over, only half expressed a preference for no work at all and most of the rest wanted part-week work all the year round (Best, 1980*a*).

Although the 'public opinion' evidence is not as extensive as in the case of flexible retirement, there is no shortage of voices putting forward the case for gradual retirement. One of the chief points is that gradual retirement helps the process of adjustment, and this is spelled out by Cannon (1968):

> One solution to the problem of adjustment to retirement is that the worker approaching retirement should slide into it gradually. At the moment the break, at whatever age it comes, tends in the majority of cases to be sharp and sudden, the contrast between employment and retirement stark. To eliminate

this we ought now to be considering schemes for allowing workers immediately over the age of retirement to work a reduced number of hours each week and to continue on a scale whereby they would work fewer and fewer hours per week until the time had come for complete retirement.

Concern about the psychological problems of adjustment to retirement is echoed by doctors who are aware that many older workers tend to resist abrupt and unplanned retirement and who therefore advocate a policy of phased retirement (Odell, 1959). Another point is that during the period of partial retirement the individual may be able to develop additional interests outside his job and thus be better prepared to continue an active life than if he had been confronted with a sudden loss of all his job responsibilities. The self-employed person who can taper off his work load is fortunate in this respect, as is the craftsman who can move from full-time employment to pursuing his trade in semi-retirement for the benefit of relatives and friends.

A sizeable minority of people prefer to retire completely rather than gradually, and they no doubt have good reasons for expressing this preference. It will be remembered that Meg, our ex-civil servant, found it desirable to change to part-time hours before retiring completely, while Norman, the ex-director, was able to jump happily, albeit with substantial monetary and personal resources, into complete retirement. The point is that individuals ought to be offered the choice of retiring gradually or completely according to their needs and interests.

A number of different suggestions have been made about ways of implementing policies of gradual retirement. The most common proposal is that older workers can move from being full-time to part-time to retiring completely, with the part-time element being fewer hours a day, fewer days per week, or (less commonly) fewer weeks per year. Another proposal, perhaps more attractive to employers than to workers, is that after full-time employment ceases the older worker can be put in a pool of temporary workers who, for example, could be standby replacements for absent regular employees, and thereby have some choice in limiting their hours or days of work.

Various part-earnings, part-pension proposals for gradual

161

retirement have attracted some interest. For example, an article in *Pre-Retirement Choice* (1975) advocated that, 'at 60 a chap should be given the chance to go onto a four-day week – drawing a fifth of his state pension and four-fifths of his pay – then at 61 onto a three-day week, and so on. At 65 you would please yourself whether you went on working or not.' The Swedish partial-pension scheme actually puts this idea into practice, and is founded on the principle that workers aged 60–65 should be allowed to reduce their hours of work and draw partial pensions as a preparation for full retirement (Bratthall, 1976).

A survey of flexible (including gradual) retirement possibilities in Belgium, Germany, France, Japan, Norway, Sweden and the United Kingdom showed that some progress (though one may argue not enough) has been made to provide older workers with more options in electing to reduce or stop work at an age suited to personal needs and circumstance (Tracy, 1978). Support for this idea has been forthcoming from the International Labour Office (1979), which believes that measures should be taken to ensure that, in a framework allowing for a gradual transition from working life to freedom of activity, retirement is, as far as possible, voluntary.

Flexible Lifestyles

Ideas and proposals – and to a limited extent achievements – regarding more flexible and gradual retirement policies may be regarded as one example of the principle of flexibility which could be applied at periods of life other than the change from work to retirement. During the last decade a number of writers have been arguing that one answer to a number of social and economic problems, and one way of improving the general quality of life, is for there to be more flexibility of opportunity in moving to and from education, work and leisure. These writers point to the present system of rigid demarcation between these spheres as having both individual and social costs: people pay heavily in missed opportunities for personal growth, and society pays in the form of job malaise, reduced productivity and diminished creativity (Jones, 1977).

The principle of flexible lifestyles is based on contrasting the present predominantly linear life patterns with those possible if the rigid division of life into periods of education, work and leisure is broken down and choice according to personal needs and circumstances becomes the guiding principle. At present most of us spend roughly the first two decades of our lives in formal education, and for many of us that is the last contact we have with 'education'. Then we work for perhaps forty years, with relatively little time for developing those leisure interests which are supposed to sustain us through the final period of life – retirement.

The essence of the principle of flexible lifestyles is 'social and economic policies that provide adults of all ages with a range of options for work, education, and free-time activities' (Havighurst, 1969). Revolutionary as this formulation may seem, it is, in reality, still based on the idea that work, education and leisure are distinguishable parts of life with their own characteristic institutions. An even more advanced formulation is that of Iyer (1966), who writes of 'the principle of simultaneity of pursuit of education, work and leisure during the whole of a man's life in the new society . . . work would become voluntary, training for, and enjoyment of, leisure a continuous activity linked with a philosophy of life-long education. If this seems a far cry from our present segregated life patterns, we need not imagine that in the medium to long term it is impossible, given the direction of changes that have already taken place.

One of the most prolific protagonists of flexible lifestyles is Best (1973, 1979, 1980*b*). He traces the need for more flexibility to a recent trend in advanced industrial societies which is that for most people the work years are being compressed into an ever-smaller portion of mid-life, while non-work time (schooling and retirement) has been growing rapidly in youth and old age. He believes that we have reached a point in the development of society where it is feasible and desirable to allow increased individualisation in all aspects of life. Needs and preferences concerning combinations of work, income and free time are a highly individual matter, and so we should seek to move towards more flexibility in when people choose to work, to be in learning situations or pursue free-time interests.

163

Writers on flexible lifestyles tend to see work as the key sphere for change, leading to consequent changes in the spheres of education and leisure. Thus Gore (1976) believes that 'much more flexible ideas about employment will have to be worked out. Part-time work, longer annual holidays, secondments and exchanges may all help to refresh older workers without resorting to the guillotine of abrupt and total retirement at a fixed age.' In advocating 'sabbaticals for all', particularly during the latter period of normal working life, Goyder (1977) suggests that sabbaticals plus flexible retirement will be of great value in promoting equity and may also enable the economy to provide work for all at some but not all stages of life by enabling people to spend more time engaged in other activities throughout their life span.

Why not provide for work, leisure and education at all ages? Older people and new parents could be allowed to work part-time and others could work full-time as their energies and needs allow. Health, motivation and economic needs should determine the amount of time worked, not chronological age. The Manpower and Social Affairs Committee of OECD has expressed the view that 'increased possibilities for individual choice should be available as between leisure and work, particularly for mature and older workers. Flexibility in this sense would also be in line with changes as to working capacity and energy associated with aging' (OECD, 1971).

Such changes as these require a more relaxed attitude to work than many of us – particularly the elderly – have today. What is wanted is not an attitude of detachment from work but a recognition that it is only part of a well-rounded life. Lefkowitz (1979) is on the right track in urging people to act on their own behalf and to be prepared to move – psychologically as well as physically – at their own wish: 'Work is like any other convenient shelter. You stay as long as it's comfortable. When things begin to break down, when the paint starts to peel, when roaches invade the kitchen, you move. Sometimes you purposely let things fall apart . . . Movement is more important than destination.' Too many people today are in sub-standard work, work from which they can see no easy way to move. Society has the resources to develop better work, not just as a shelter from a meaningless life, but as a gateway to worthwhile leisure and educational experiences.

Provision of Work

A central theme of this book is that, while many older people are happy and fulfilled in retirement, many others are not, and that their main need is to remain active and useful members of society through playing a work role of some kind. It is encouraging that the Department of Health and Social Security (1978) in its policy discussion document has posed the question: 'What encouragement should be given to the extension of opportunities for work after retirement?' 'Work' does not necessarily mean employment and in a society which, in the short run at least, is making employment increasingly difficult to obtain, it is necessary to find or create types of work that do not rely on the conventional relationship of employee to employer.

One of the goals gerontology has been described as assuring that older people who need work, want work and who are fitted for work are given an equal opportunity with others to obtain work (Abrams, 1955). It is abundantly clear that there are men and women approaching mandatory retirement age who would undertake jobs if they were available. The campaign to provide for the continued employment of older workers is no new one, as the following statement by the National Advisory Committee on the Employment of Older Men and Women (1953) testifies:

> We attach the utmost importance to efforts to promote the continuance of older persons, still fit and able to work, in their existing employment ... All men and women employed in industry, commerce, the professions, or elsewhere, who can give effective service, either in their normal work or on any alternative work which their employers can make available, should be given the opportunity, without regard to age, to continue at work if they so wish.

Of course, this was written in the period of 'discouraged' retirement, when there was still a shortage of labour rather than of jobs. But older people who need work are still with us, and it is a condemnation of our social and economic system that it is not able to provide suitable work for those men and women of all ages who need it.

The case for providing suitable work for those older people who want it rests partly on medical grounds. We have seen in Chapter 5 that, while retirement can have a beneficial effect on the physical health of some kinds of worker, it can also have an adverse effect on the mental health of others. Many older people do not want to retire, and if they have to they tend to become despondent at the timelessness and aimlessness which retirement can bring (Oldfield, 1968). The weight of medical opinion is that sudden disuse of mental and bodily functions, previously regularly exercised, such as may happen through retirement, is likely to cause atrophy and degeneration (Shenfield, 1957). However, it does not follow that continued paid employment of the elderly is necessarily the only or the best way to avoid this, or that leisure or other non-work pursuits cannot equally nourish vitality in old age.

If it is accepted that many older people do need work in some form, the question arises: What kind of work? There is no shortage of suggestions, though some of the kinds of work proposed are probably acceptable to only a few older people. Older workers tend to be more common in non-manufacturing forms of industry, and one suggestion is to reinforce this trend by encouraging more older workers into non-manufacturing or service work, thus releasing more able-bodied workers for manufacturing industries (Jenkins, 1973). This proposal loses some of its force when we consider that technological advances are bringing 'manufacturing' work well within the physical capability of older workers.

Some of the suggestions for providing work for older people are made with a view to their not competing for jobs with younger workers, while other writers are more concerned about the special needs of older workers. Loudoun (1977) believes that there are many ways in which retired people can make use of their experience without taking away the jobs of younger people, and she mentions the need for them in charitable organisations and in supplementing the social services. Lishman (1975) thinks

166

that the use of older people as a resource by working mothers or by schools needs to be explored much beyond the links which already exist within family groups. According to Aiken (1978) 'elderly people could staff day-care centres and kindergartens, work on historical projects and crafts, and even become small-scale food producers by operating abandoned farms'. The Joneses' (1973) list of tasks for the elderly centre around cultural provision and environmental improvement: founding and supporting local historical societies, reviving local customs, reactivating local crafts, beautifying the environment, acting as library aides, anti-pollution volunteers, giving para-professional help to nurses and doctors.

More generally, Townsend (1957) is among those who advocate a policy of sheltered workshops for the elderly, so that they can work at a pace that suits them and not compete on unfavourable terms with younger workers. The danger here is low rates of pay for those designated as inferior workers. But whatever the form of the work provided, it is clear that a lead needs to be given nationally. Neighbourhood councils of the retired and local branches of such bodies as Age Concern, together with educational authorities, social service departments, voluntary bodies and area health authorities can review local needs and possible uses of the retired in meeting those needs.

Some ocupations lend themselves to continued involvement after formal retirement, sometimes for a different client or customer group. Thus retired lawyers can offer legal services to the aged, retired teachers can give courses, and retired doctors and nurses can supply home medical care. This kind of continuity in a profession or kind of work is better than offering old people what may appear to them to be trivial or inconsequential tasks just to keep them occupied. 'Foster grandparents' schemes, for example, appeal to some, but are a futile if not insulting solution to the problems of retired people with some professional or manual skill which they wish to continue exercising (Jaffe, 1972).

In the long run, the prospects for useful employment of older people are reasonably good. At present older workers tend to be employed in rather less skilled occupations than younger

167

workers, but the gradual occupational upgrading of the older labour force that appears to be taking place is encouraging. There is every indication that the proportion of white-collar and professional workers in the older labour force will continue to rise in the future, as the large numbers of young people now in these types of work move into the older age groups. This will probably mean somewhat enhanced job security for older workers.

There is clear evidence from surveys of the need for part-time work among the elderly, often as part of a preferred pattern of gradual retirement. Part-time employment can be of particular value to retirees who do not require to work full-time for economic reasons but who could benefit economically, and in other ways, from part-time work. Men and women who are fit enough should, if they wish, be able to have two part-time jobs rather than one full-time job. Not only would this enable those with varied talents and interests to exercise more than one of these, but it would also make gradual retirement more possible by enabling one of the part-time jobs to be given up while the other is retained. If we are, as some observers believe, to face an increasingly non-labour intensive society, then part-time work for all, rather than full-time work for some, may become a practical and desirable proposition.

Some employers are reluctant to employ people part-time: they worry about administrative complications and the increase in their social security burden. With the intention of resolving this last difficulty, the French government decided a few years ago that to employ two persons part-time to do the job of one full-time employee should not entail greater social security contributions and family allowances from the employer than those incurred by the employment of one full-time worker. This is a useful step in the right direction which other countries would do well to emulate, but it must be accompanied by a greater willingness on the part of both employees and employers to view part-time work as something to be encouraged rather than looked upon as an exception to the full-time rule.

A variant of part-time work is the concept of job-sharing. There is no good reason why older people should not be able to say, 'I like my job and want to carry on doing it for many years, but I would like to share it with somebody else'. Job-sharing means that two (or possibly more) people would share the responsibility for getting a certain amount of work done or services rendered, but it would allow the sharers more flexibility in deciding their work schedules than if they had separate jobs.

The concept of a second or third career is another contribution to solving the problem of what kind of work should be provided for the elderly. Men and women can 'retire' from one type of work and take up another – perhaps in a completely different field and perhaps also after a period of training. Already some older people are fortunate enough to have such opportunities, but we need to make many more available in order not to waste human potential and not to frustrate the desire for useful and interesting work. Mid-career clinics or other institutional arrangements have been suggested for making it possible to change type of work in later life (Eisdorfer, 1978). Not only is greater occupational mobility likely to result in a better match of jobs to people, but post-retirement neurosis is probably most effectively cured by the interesting activity of a new job.

The final question we have to consider in work for the elderly is: Who should do the providing? One obvious answer is that all present employing bodies – public and private, local and national, large and small – have a responsibility in this regard. It has been suggested that public measures should include the development of new fields of interest and hence of employment, such as recreational counselling, para-professional legal, health and social services, and small-scale production such as 'cottage industries' and handicrafts (Stagner, 1978). Another long-standing proposal is for government-subsidised workshops and self-help co-operatives. Since many older people want part-time local work, there is a case for setting up locally based public agencies which can find, negotiate for and create work for those who wish to avail themselves of the opportunity. There are a large number of organisations – social, political, charitable, religious – which could offer work to retired people, either without payment beyond expenses or for a little pin money if need be.

The issue of work versus retirement for elderly people involves all those aspects of management, union and government policy that affect the decisions and possibilities of older people to work or not. Policies affecting the hiring and retention of older workers, the adequacy of public and private pension schemes, the earnings rule limit on pensions (or the retirement test, as it is called in the USA, retirement preparation and educational programmes are all closely related to the problem. A less direct but even more important influence on whether we give those older people who want to work the opportunity to do so is our whole approach to the social and economic ordering of our society, and the place of work in it.

The Role of Education

We can formulate policies for work, others for leisure, and yet others for education. But in our increasingly complex society each of these policies inevitably affects and is affected by the others. In this section I want to deal with the role of education at three successively more general levels: education for retirement, education as an interest in retirement, and education as a means of understanding the possibilities for development and change inherent in our society and in our own lives.

Education already plays a significant part in preparing some men and women for retirement, and there is good reason to believe that it should play a greater part in the future. As we saw in Chapter 3, very few people today attend any kind of pre-retirement course, and if they do make a satisfactory adjustment to retirement it is thanks more to their own attitudes and determination than to the availability of educational courses devoted to retirement preparation. The most effective type of retirement preparation seems to be based on participative, 'round table' methods rather than purely on 'top table' instructive methods.

Both individual and group services should be available, and over a much longer period than just before retirement. Group discussions might well start five to ten years before retirement and be continued in periodic discussions or concentrated courses until people actually retire. Individual counselling services could be made available, either separately or linked to the group services.

If one theme is education for retirement, then another is certainly retirement as education – the two are, in fact, closely linked. Some retirees already avail themselves of educational opportunities as a means of using their time in both an interesting and pleasurable way. Evenings at the ivory tower are, as Jary (1973) points out, vastly underestimated as sources of pleasant companionship and disinterested leisurely learning – in the case of retirees the evenings can extend to mornings and afternoons, and the subjects can be anything from philosophy to dancing, from macramé to car maintenance. In addition, adult education provides many chances to experiment with, to sample and to develop secondary interests and possible careers to take the place of what is lost on retirement. As R. F. W. Smith (1957) puts it, most important of all education provides a continuing acquaintance with the world of ideas, with literature, art, music and the considerations of philosophy that are, in the last analysis, the only real preparation for life, for retirement and for death.

There are pros and cons of providing lifelong education in the form of mixing the age groups or of educational institutions run for, and by, older people, institutions which acknowledge that their needs are qualitatively different from the more instrumental goals of younger people in our society. My own view is that there is more to be gained than lost by encouraging a mix of the age groups. Although mental responses tend to slow and perceptions diminish with age, these decrements are compensated for by the older person's wider range of knowledge and experience. At all ages we should be recognising the value of education. Employment is not enough to make a whole life because it may one day come to an end. Home is not enough, because children grow and depart, and domesticity itself becomes a settled routine. Entertainments are not enough, because mind and body crave some purposeful occupation. The element lacking in each of these facets of life, worthwhile though they may be up to a point, is one or more absorbing personal interests that can grow in strength to fill the vacuum of old age (Groombridge, 1960).

The third area for education is the more radical one of seeking to understand the possibilities for development and change relating particularly to the role of the elderly in our society.

Older people are often denied fulfilling lives because they perceive, quite correctly in the context of prevailing policies towards the elderly, that they should go quietly towards death and not disturb the *status quo* by asking for more. As Pyke (1980) scathingly remarks, 'the old are to be supported in comfort and warmth; their teeth, eyes and toe-nails are to be looked after, and every second Saturday bingo is to be provided at the Darby and Joan Club'.

Education can change all this by making older people more assertive of their rights to full participation in society rather than passively to accept a 'disengaged' status. A full life is open, ever-changing, never finally set. The achievement of realisable change depends on the quality of education available and on the degree of enlightenment by which people collectively order their environment and behave at every age.

Policies for Leisure

If one major theme of this book is that many older people need a useful working role in society, another is that we should all feel less guilty about having leisure than many of us do. It may be the sign of a well-integrated life that someone does not demand more leisure, or even talk about leisure very much – it probably means that he has the kind of work ('commitment' would be a better term) that gives him the satisfactions that many of us are forced to seek in our non-work time. Nevertheless, leisure, in the form of freely chosen activities or simply 'being', is an integral part of the good life and needs to be studied, planned for if necessary, and certainly enjoyed, just as work and education are studied, planned for and (if we are lucky) enjoyed.

There are several approaches to leisure which serve to reinforce those aspects of social attitudes and organisation – compulsory retirement, uniform treatment of non-uniform people, rigid demarcation of roles, and linear rather than flexible lifestyles – which I have been critically evaluating. One such approach is to hold that retirement is the time to do nothing more than to sit back and enjoy leisure. To criticise this is not to imply that retirement should not include being a time for leisure.

It is simply to assert that there is no good reason why the benefits of leisure should be deferred until the time when one ceases employment. If we embrace a policy of providing suitable work for all who need it irrespective of age, and a policy of life-long education irrespective of age, then it follows that leisure is no longer an experience, or a set of activities or interests which are to be confined to any one period of life.

A second approach to leisure which limits human potentiality is to define it only as a product or consequence of work. Leisure as conditional upon work, as a reward for work, is less likely to be seen as something valuable in its own right than if it is located as a sphere of life and of society which interacts with, rather than is dependent upon, other spheres. Thirdly, if leisure is defined only as the opposite of work, and if retirement is the opposite of work, then the scene is set for the traumatic change from full-time work to its opposite condition of retirement which so many men and women have to endure today. Retirement and leisure both have a low status because we are still a work-oriented society. But the collapse of work (Jenkins and Sherman, 1979) is going to face us with the challenge of more positively evaluating all its 'opposites', including unemployment, retirement and leisure. Work-sharing, longer holidays, shorter working weeks and earlier retirement – from employment but not necessarily from work – are all useful reforms but if they are effectively to improve the quality of life they must be accompanied by more revolutionary changes in attitudes, especially in relation to leisure.

A particularly desirable step, and one which has far-reaching implications for the integration of work and leisure, is the concept of sabbaticals for all. The sabbatical is more than a somewhat longer than usual period of leisure: it implies an amount of time long enough to undertake or develop some interest which revivifies the individual, enabling him both to realise his potential in a new direction and to return to something like his pre-sabbatical work with fresh mental vigour. An extended sabbatical system would facilitate varied outlets for human energies and varied opportunities for building a fulfilling life throughout adulthood. Giving people in their early adult life more time between periods of employment to study, to learn new

173

skills, time for parents to raise a family and build a home or to travel, could enable more older people to be entrusted with the job of keeping the wheels of industry turning and providing the services needed. With working life thus extended and inter-spersed with periods of education or the pursuit of leisure interests, the popular goal of gradual and flexible retirement could be achieved.

Apart from the timing of leisure and trying to make sure that substantial periods of it are not deferred until normal retirement age, there is the question of whether policies for leisure should seek to encourage men and women to spend their free time in some particular kinds of ways rather than others. An important part of the work ethic is that leisure – preferably conceived of more narrowly as 'recreation' and with the temptation to add 'wholesome' – should serve the function of re-creating the individual for the next period of work. Retirement, in this perspective, is seen as the ultimate reward for a lifetime of work. Concern is sometimes expressed about the ways in which people choose to spend their leisure time, though today this concern is more likely to be for the well-being of the individual rather than for economic or functional considerations. Thus Dumazedier and Ripert (1963) have posed the question: 'So far as leisure is concerned, is it better to encourage older people to continue activities connected with work and various obligations . . . or to spend more time in complete relaxation?'

In a liberal democracy that claims to put the well-being of individuals above sectional or collective interests such as those of employers or the state, the answer to such questions must be: people of all ages should be encouraged to 'do their own thing', provided that this is not detrimental to the well-being of others. This is not to say that we need no policies for leisure. We need to provide people with the means of having the kind of leisure lives they prefer, including information enabling them to see that they have a choice. This could include, for example, encouraging the growth of associational and club life and a variety of cultural pursuits among the elderly. No value judgements about taste need be implied – bingo is as good as Beethoven. In so far as some older people have gained many of their leisure satisfac-tions in sociable interaction with their workmates, we should find ways of avoiding the separation of men and women from their chosen work-and-leisure relationships. For those who are happy to give up all forms of work we must try to ensure that leisure is experienced as something worthwhile as well as enjoyable, and not just as a time filler.

The Future of Retirement

Finally, we come to weigh up the directions in which our society seems to be going in relation to work and retirement and to see how we might influence future developments in desired directions.

The practical base for many – but not all – things that can be done to help the elderly is financial. One element in helping to improve the financial position of the elderly is to pursue policies which stimulate the rate of economic growth and the demand for labour, thereby enabling more older workers to be employed at non-exploitive rates of pay. We could follow the example of countries such as the USSR which have adopted measures encouraging people to work past pension age and enabling them to receive both their pension and wages. Although in Britain the total cost to the state of a general fall in retirement age for men to 60 was estimated to be over £1,500 million a few years ago (Taylor, 1976) – and today would be of the order of at least £3,000 million – much of this would be offset by the continued output of healthy older workers and the transfer of others from unemployment to retirement benefits. The current moves towards earlier retirement and pension ages are largely attempts to alleviate the overall problem of unemployment by defining the older unemployed worker as retired, and in so far as retirement is not the chosen status of many of these men and women we must make sure that adequate retirement income is available.

For many years a few mostly unheeded voices have been advocating that old age should not be treated as a passive period of waiting for death, but should be seen as offering a new lease on life which, in optimum fulfilment, calls for new ways of living – ways possibly as different from those of mid-life as adolescence is from adulthood. The modern and radical expression of this point of view is the Gray Panther phenomenon in the USA, which

175

advocates that people in their later years need not remain passive and impotent in the face of unacceptable roles. Maggie Kuhn, the leader of the Gray Panthers, disdains the activities of Golden Age Clubs as 'playpens for the old' and has declared that 'we are not mellow, sweet old people. We have got to effect changes and we have nothing to lose.'

The increasing assertiveness, even militancy of at least some of the present generation of older people will in the long run necessitate appropriate responses from all sectors of society. In Britain, Len Murray, the trade union leader, has expressed his belief in a society in which retirement is regarded as a liberation, as an incentive to live actively and positively. We must not rely only on what the state and other bodies can do – there is a need for retired people themselves to take the initiative in creating the desired types of environments and attitudes for their lives in retirement.

The future of retirement is a matter, first, of understanding what are the various possible roles for older people in our society, and secondly of taking steps to see that individual choice is catered for as far as possible. The role possibilities are many, but they may be crudely dichotomised as (1) encourage retired people to live out their years in pursuit of time-filling hobbies, entertainments and in reflective vegetation, or (2) regard them as a rich source of energy, experience and wisdom, capable of attaining self-realisation and carrying, if they wish, important community responsibilities. The first alternative promises boredom, deterioration, dependency, conservatism, depression and institutionalisation. The second promises continued growth, preservation of vital functions, purposeful living, continued social usefulness and self-sufficiency.

Sheppard and Rix (1977) pose an important question: How long can we continue the downward trend in average age of retirement without nearly intolerable economic costs for the individual and for the general economy? Their answer is to choose one of three alternatives: (1) a smaller number of retirees who can maintain an acceptable retirement status, (2) more retirees who will have to live at lower than pre-retirement standards, or (3) the working population to contribute more to maintain a larger number of retirees at acceptable standards.

They see the first and second options as politically unacceptable. The first option clearly implies a non-age-discriminatory retirement policy for older workers and flexible, if not gradual, retirement.

Is it possible to find a selection of policies which will meet aspirations for flexible and earlier retirement, combined with a socially acceptable level of income for older people, yet at the same time minimise the potentially very large addition to pension costs? Fogarty (1980) is among those who believe that it is possible. There would need to be three main elements in the strategy: opportunities for gradual early retirement on part pension, selective reduction of standard or normal retirement ages, and positive inducements to continue in employment beyond, as well as up to, standard retirement age.

Much of the present unease about retirement stems from its negative associations: instead of being a positive means of self-actualisation, it is too often seen as just an anti-climax to a working life or career. We speak of retirement *from* instead of retirement *for*. Although society, through pensions and other benefits and services, provides various forms of help to the retired person, the circumstances of this help tend to rob him of his dignity, for there is little recognition that this is his due, and not a thinly disguised, and indeed sometimes overt, form of charity.

Retirement from jobs should, as far as possible, be optional according to the capabilities, needs and wishes of the person concerned. It need not mean retirement from all work, but it can certainly mean this if that is what is wanted. The policy advocated for the Canadian government by Brown (1975) can serve as a practical and humane guide for the policies of all bodies in all countries: 'It is essential that government now . . . develop policies on retirement age which recognise the wishes of the Canadian people, establish appropriate priorities, ensure maximum equity, maintain the right to work for those who wish it, and offer a worthwhile life in retirement for those who wish to retire.'

Conclusion

In the Introduction I set out to show that there are two basically different ways of approaching questions of work and retirement:

one restrictive, conformist and conservative, the other expansive, creative and radical. In previous chapters links have been traced between particular expressions of these approaches. On the one hand, we have retirement policies based on the 'needs' of the economy, the disengagement theory of ageing with the same functionalist bias, the preference to instruct people about how to prepare for retirement, stress on decrements in working abilities with age, a narrow concern with employment, and the separation of work from leisure. On the other hand, we have retirement policies based on the needs of people, the activity theory with a bias to continuity of lifestyle, the encouragement of people to participate actively in their own retirement preparation, stress on combating the prejudices of ageism, a wider concern with work, and the integration of work with leisure.

In this final chapter we have considered several further manifestations of the two contrasting approaches. Restriction, conformity and conservatism are represented by fixed-age retirement policies, compulsory and complete retirement, and linear lifestyles. Expansion, creativity and radicalism are represented by flexible retirement policies, voluntary and gradual retirement, and flexible lifestyles.

In all this we may trace a mutual influence of theory, practice, attitude and policy. Alternative general theories about the economy and society link with more specific theories about the ageing process and the relation of work and leisure. Retirement preparation practices and attitudes to education, work and leisure feed into work and retirement policies and are, in turn, modified by the implementation of some of these policies and not others. Ultimately the test of the adequacy of the theories and policies, and the justification of the attitudes and practices, consist in the experiences of people, measured principally by surveys and case studies and interpreted in the light of all we know about social processes with their many manifestations and possibilities.

From a humanistic standpoint it seems to me generally preferable to choose the path of expansion, creativity and radicalism rather than of restriction, conformity and conservatism. But this proposition should not be elevated to dogma. There are circumstances in which contrary options may be preferable: occasions, for example, when disengagement is appropriate, when age decrements have to be recognised as real and unavoidable in their consequences, and when to retire completely is better than to seek to do so gradually. But I believe that the alternative options to these are generally more in line with the direction of human development, at a period in our history when old ideas about education, work and leisure are being challenged and when the advancing applications of technology are helping us to redefine what machines can be made to do and human beings should be free to do.

Bibliography

Abrams, A. J. (1955), 'Discrimination against older workers in various countries', in *Report of the Third Congress of the International Association of Gerontology, London 1954* (Edinburgh: Livingstone).

Abrams, M. (1978), 'Time and the elderly', *New Society* (21 December).

Abrams, M. (1979), 'The future of the elderly', *Futures*, vol. 11 (June).

Abrams, M. (1980), *Beyond Three-Score and Ten* (London: Age Concern).

Achenbaum, A. (1974), 'The obsolescence of old age in America 1865–1914', *Journal of Social History*, vol. 7 (Fall).

Achenbaum, A. (1978), *Old Age in the New Land* (Baltimore, Md: Johns Hopkins University Press).

Acuff, G., and Allen, D. (1970), 'Hiatus in meaning: disengagement for retired professors', *Journal of Gerontology*, vol. 25 (April).

Adams, D. (1980), 'No regrets for my lost job', *Pre-Retirement Choice* (April).

Age Concern (1974), *The Attitudes of the Retired and the Elderly* (London: Age Concern).

Age Concern Today (1974), 'Industry and the retired', no. 10 (Summer).

Aiken, L. (1978), *Later Life* (Philadelphia, Penn.: Saunders).

Anderson, J. E. (1958), 'Psychological aspects of the use of free time', in W. Donahue *et al.* (eds), *Free Time: Challenge to Later Maturity* (Ann Arbor, Mich.: University of Michigan Press).

Anderson, W. F. (1969), 'Preparation for retirement', *Transactions of the Society of Occupational Medicine*, vol. 19.

Anderson, W. F. (1970), 'Future planning of retirement policies', *Gerontology*, vol. 1 (April).

Anderson, W. F. and Cowan, N. R. (1956), 'Work and retirement: influences on the health of older men', *Lancet* (29 December).

Ash, P. (1966), 'Pre-retirement counseling', *Gerontologist*, vol. 6 (June).

Atchley, R. C. (1971*a*), 'Disengagement among professors', *Journal of Gerontology*, vol. 26 (October).

Atchley, R. C. (1971*b*), 'Retirement and leisure participation: continuity or crisis?', *Gerontologist*, vol. 11 (Spring).

Atchley, R. C. (1972), *The Social Forces in Later Life* (Belmont, Calif.: Wadsworth).

Atchley, R. C. (1975), 'Adjustment to loss of job at retirement', *Aging and Human Development*, vol. 6, no. 1.

Atchley, R. C. (1976), *The Sociology of Retirement* (New York: Schenkman).

Atchley, R. C. (1979), 'Issues in retirement research', *Gerontologist*, vol. 19 (February).

Atkinson, A. M. (1970), 'Occupation in retirement', *Gerontology*, vol. 1 (April).

Back, K. W. (1969), 'The ambiguity of retirement', in E. W. Busse and E. P. Pfeiffer (eds), *Behavior and Adaptation in Late Life* (Boston, Mass.: Little, Brown).

Bibliography

Barr, P. (n.d.), 'Occupation and leisure', in *The Place of the Retired and Elderly in Modern Society* (London: Age Concern).

Barrett, J. H. (1972), *Gerontological Psychology* (Springfield, Ill.: C. C. Thomas).

Barron, M. L. (1961), *The Aging American* (New York: Crowell).

Bauder, W. W., and Doerflinger, J. P. (1967), 'Work roles among the rural retired', in E. G. Youmans (ed.), *Older Rural Americans* (Lexington, Ky: University of Kentucky Press).

Baum, M., and Baum, R. C. (1980), *Growing Old* (Englewood Cliffs, NJ: Prentice-Hall).

Beauvoir, S. de (1972), *Old Age* (London: Deutsch).

Belbin, R. M. (1953), 'Difficulties of older people in industry', *Occupational Psychology*, vol. 27 (July).

Belbin, R. M. (1972), 'Retirement strategy in an evolving society', in F. M. Carp (ed.), *The Retirement Process* (Washington, DC: US Government Printing Office).

Belbin, R. M. (1973), 'New trends in retirement', *Proceedings of the Royal Society of Medicine*, vol. 66 (August).

Belbin, R. M., and Clark, F. le Gros (1970), 'The relationship between retirement patterns and work as revealed by the British census', *Industrial Gerontology*, vol. 4 (Winter).

Bengston, V. L., Chiribosa, D. A., and Keller, A. B. (1969), 'Occupational differences in retirement', in R. J. Havighurst *et al.* (eds), *Adjustment to Retirement* (Assen: Van Gorcum).

Berglind, H. (1978), 'Early retirement pensions in Sweden: trends and regional variations', *Scandinavian Journal of Social Medicine*, vol. 6, no. 1.

Best, F. (1973), 'Flexible work scheduling: beyond the forty-hour impasse', in F. Best (ed.), *The Future of Work* (Englewood Cliffs, NJ: Prentice-Hall).

Best, F. (1979), 'The future of retirement and lifetime distribution of work', *Aging and Work*, vol. 2 (Summer).

Best, F. (1980*a*), *Exchanging Earnings for Leisure: Findings of an Exploratory National Survey on Work Time Preferences* (Washington, DC: US Government Printing Office).

Best, F. (1980*b*), *Flexible Life Scheduling* (New York: Praeger).

Beveridge, W. (1942), *Social Insurance and Allied Services*, Cmd 6404 (London: HMSO).

Beveridge, W. E. (1965), 'How worthwhile is retirement?', *New Society* (3 June).

Beveridge, W. E. (1968), 'Problems in preparing for retirement', in H. B. Wright (ed.), *Solving the Problems of Retirement* (London: Institute of Directors).

Beveridge, W. E. (1980), 'Retirement and life significance', *Human Relations*, vol. 33, no. 1.

Bixby, L. (1976), 'Retirement patterns in the United States', *Social Security Bulletin*, vol. 39 (August).

Blaire, T. (1977), 'In practice', *Community Care* (20 July).

Blaxter, M. (1976), *The Meaning of Disability* (London: Heinemann).

Blitsten, D. R. (1963), *The World of the Family* (New York: Random House).

Bratthall, K. (1976), 'Flexible retirement and the new Swedish partial-pension scheme', *Industrial Gerontology*, vol. 3 (Summer).

Breckinridge, E. L. (1953), *Effective Use of the Older Workers* (Chicago: Wilcox & Follet).

Breen, L. Z. (1963), 'Retirement – norms, behaviour and functional aspects of normative behaviour', in R. H. Williams *et al.* (eds), *Processes of Aging* (Englewood Cliffs, NJ: Prentice-Hall).

Brehm, H. P. (1968), 'Sociology and aging: orientation and research', *Gerontologist*, vol. 8 (Spring).

Brown, J. C. (1975), *How Much Choice? Retirement Policies in Canada* (Canadian Council on Social Development).

Brown, R. G., McKeown, T., and Whitfield, A. G. W. (1958), 'Observations on the medical condition of men in the seventh decade', *British Medical Journal* (8 March).

Butler, R. N. (1972), 'A life-cycle perspective: public policies for later life', in F. M. Carp (ed.), *Retirement* (New York: Behavioural Publications).

Cain, L. (1967), 'Age status and generational phenomena', *Gerontologist*, vol. 7 (June).

Cameron, N. (1945), 'Neuroses of later maturity', in O. J. Kaplan (ed.), *Mental Disorders in Later Life* (Stanford, Calif.: Stanford University Press).

Cannon, L. (1968), 'A trade union leader's view on the problems of retirement', in H. B. Wright (ed.), *Solving the Problems of Retirement* (London: Institute of Directors).

Carp, F. M. (ed.) (1968), *The Retirement Process* (Washington, DC: US Government Printing Office).

Cesa-Bianchi, M., *et al.* (1969), 'Post-retirement patterns in Milan', in R. J. Havighurst *et al.* (eds), *Adjustment to Retirement* (Atlantic Highlands, NJ: Humanities Press).

Chown, S. M., and Heron, A. (1965), 'Psychological aspects of ageing in man', *Annual Review of Psychology*.

Christ, E. A. (1965), 'The "retired" stamp collector: economic and other functions of systematized leisure activity', in A. Rose and W. Peterson (eds), *Older People and their Social World* (Philadelphia, Penn.: Davis).

Christrup, H., and Thurman, C. (1973), 'A preretirement program that works', *Journal of Home Economics*, vol. 65.

Clark, F. le Gros (1973), 'Employment for the retired', *Age Concern Today*, no. 5 (Spring).

Clark, F. le Gros, and Dunne, A. C. (1955), *Ageing in Industry* (London: Nuffield Foundation).

Clark, M. (1972), 'An anthropological view of retirement', in F. M. Carp (ed.), *Retirement* (New York: Behavioural Publications).

Clark, M., and Anderson, B. (1967), *Culture and Aging* (Springfield, Ill.: C. C. Thomas).

Cole, S. (1979), 'Age and scientific performance', *American Journal of Sociology*, vol. 84 (January).

Cooley, L. F., and L. M. (1965), *The Retirement Trap* (Garden City, NY: Doubleday).

Bibliography

Comfort, A. (1976), *A Good Age* (London: Mitchell Beazley).

Corson, J. H., and McConnell, J. W. (1956), *Economic Needs of Older People* (New York: Twentieth Century Fund).

Council of Europe (1977), *Preparation for Retirement* (Strasbourg: Council of Europe).

Cowgill, D. O. (1976), 'A previous incarnation of disengagement theory', *Gerontology*, vol. 4 (August).

Cowgill, D. O., and Baulch, N. (1962), 'The use of leisure time by older people', *Gerontologist*, vol. 2 (March).

Crawford, M. P. (1971), 'Retirement and disengagement', *Human Relations*, vol. 24, no. 3.

Crawford, M. P. (1972*a*), 'Retirement and role playing', *Sociology*, vol. 6, no. 2.

Crawford, M. P. (1972*b*), 'Retirement as a psycho-social crisis', *Journal of Psychosomatic Research*, vol. 16.

Crawford, M. P. (1973), 'Retirement: a *rite de passage*', *Sociological Review*, vol. 21 (August).

Cumming, E. M., and Henry, W. (1961), *Growing Old* (New York: Basic Books).

Cunningham, D. A., Montoye, H. J., Metzner, H. L., and Keller, J. B. (1968), 'Active leisure time activities as related to age among males in a total population', *Journal of Gerontology*, vol. 23 (October).

Daniel, W. W. (1974), *A National Survey of the Unemployed* (London: PEP).

Daric, J. (1955), 'Survey of the employment of elderly workers in France', in *Report of the Third Congress of the International Association of Gerontology, London 1954* (Edinburgh: Livingstone).

Dennis, W. (1966), 'Creative productivity between the ages of 20 and 80 years', *Journal of Gerontology*, vol. 21 (January).

Department of Education and Science (1973), *Adult Education: A Plan for Development* (Russell Report) (London: HMSO).

Department of Health and Social Security (1978), *A Happier Old Age* (London: HMSO).

Desai, K. G., and Naik, R. D. (1974), *Problems of Retired People in Greater Bombay* (Bombay: Tara Institute of Social Sciences).

Donovan, R. J., and Associates Pty Ltd (1978), *Survey of Leisure Activities, Interests, Opinions and Concerns of Pre-Retired and Retired* (Perth: Community Recreation Council of Western Australia).

Draper, J. E., Lundgren, E. F., and Strother, G. B. (1967), *Work Attitudes and Retirement Adjustment* (Madison, Wis.: University of Wisconsin Bureau of Business Research and Service).

Dumazedier, J., and Ripert, A. (1963), 'Retirement and leisure', *International Social Science Journal*, vol. 15.

Dunbar, J. (1976), *Into Retirement* (London: Arrow Books).

Eisdorfer, C. (1978), 'Societal response to aging: some possible consequences', in L. F. Jarvik (ed.), *Aging into the 21st Century* (New York: Gardner Press).

Emerson, A. R. (1959), 'The first year of retirement', *Occupational Psychology*, vol. 33 (October).

Estes, C. L. (1978), 'The politics of aging', *Society*, vol. 15 (July).

Epstein, L. A., and Murray, J. H. (1968), 'Employment and retirement', in B. L. Neugarten (ed.), *Middle Age and Aging* (Chicago: Chicago University Press).

Evans, W. (n.d.), *Need I Ever Retire?* (London: Chest and Heart Association).

Fengler, A. P. (1975), 'Attitudinal orientations of wives toward their husbands' retirement', *Aging and Human Development*, vol. 6, no. 2.

Fillenbaum, G. G. (1971*a*), 'On the relation between attitude to work and attitude to retirement', *Journal of Gerontology*, vol. 26 (April).

Fillenbaum, G. G. (1971*b*), 'Retirement planning programs: at what age and for whom?', *Gerontologist*, vol. 11 (Spring).

Fillenbaum, G. G., and Maddox, G. L. (1974), 'Work after retirement', *Gerontologist*, vol. 14 (October).

Fischer, D. H. (1977), *Growing Old in America* (New York: Oxford University Press).

Fleming, C. E. (1962), 'The age factor in the Sheffield cutlery industry', in C. Tibbitts and W. Donahue (eds), *Social and Psychological Aspects of Aging* (New York: Columbia University Press).

Fogarty, M. (1975), *40 to 60: How We Waste the Middle Aged* (London: Centre for Studies in Social Policy).

Fogarty, M. (1980), *Retirement Age and Retirement Costs* (London: Policy Studies Institute).

Fox, A. J. (1979), 'The role of OPCS in occupational epidemiology: some examples', *Annals of Occupational Hygiene*, vol. 21.

Fox, J. H. (1977), 'Effects of retirement and former work life on women's adaptation in old age', *Journal of Gerontology*, vol. 32 (March).

Fried, E. G. (1949), 'Attitudes of the older population groups towards activity and inactivity', *Journal of Gerontology*, vol. 4 (April).

Friedmann, E. A. (1958), 'The work of leisure', in W. Donahue *et al.* (eds), *Free Time: Challenge to Later Maturity* (Ann Arbor, Mich.: University of Michigan Press).

Friedmann, E. A., and Havighurst, R. J. (1954), *The Meaning of Work and Retirement* (Chicago: Chicago University Press).

Friedmann, E. A., and Orbach, H. L. (1974), 'Adjustment to retirement', in S. Arieti (ed.), *American Handbook of Psychiatry*, Vol. 1 (New York: Basic Books).

Geist, H. (1968), *The Psychological Aspects of Retirement* (Springfield, Ill.: C. C. Thomas).

General Household Survey, 1979 (1980) (London: HMSO).

George, L. K. (1974), 'The impact of retirement on morale; a longitudinal study', *Gerontologist*, vol. 14 (October).

Ginzberg, E. (1979), *Good Jobs, Bad Jobs, No Jobs* (Cambridge, Mass.: Harvard University Press).

Ginzberg, E., and Herma, J. (1964), *Talent and Performance* (New York: Columbia University Press).

Glamser, F. D., and DeJong, G. F. (1975), 'The efficacy of preretirement preparation programs for industrial workers', *Journal of Gerontology*, vol. 30 (September).

Bibliography

Glenn, N. D. (1969), 'Aging, disengagement and opinionation', *Public Opinion Quarterly*, vol. 33 (Spring).

Gordon, M. S. (1964), *National Retirement Policies and the Displaced Older Worker* (Berkeley, Calif.: University of California Press).

Gore, I. (1976), *The Generation Jigsaw* (London: Allen & Unwin).

Goudy, W. J., Powers, E. A., and Keith, P. (1975), 'Work and retirement: a test of attitudinal relationships', *Journal of Gerontology*, vol. 30 (March).

Goyder, C. (1977), *Sabbaticals for All* (London: NCLC Publishing Society).

Griffiths, T. (1973), *Enjoy Your Retirement* (Newton Abbot: David & Charles).

Groombridge, B. (1960), *Education and Retirement* (London: National Institute of Adult Education).

Gubrium, J. F. (1974), *Late Life: Communities and Environmental Policy* (Springfield, Ill.: C. C. Thomas).

Hall, H. (1960), 'To retire or not?', in C. Tibbitts and W. Donahue (eds), *Aging in Today's Society* (Englewood Cliffs, NJ: Prentice-Hall).

Hansen, G. D., Yoshioka, S., Taves, M. J., and Caro, F. (1965), 'Older people in the Midwest: conditions and attitudes', in A. M. Rose and W. A. Peterson (eds), *Older People and their Social World* (Philadelphia, Penn.: Davis).

Harris, A., and Parker, S. (1973), 'Leisure and the elderly', in M. A. Smith *et al.* (eds), *Leisure and Society in Britain* (London: Allen Lane).

Harrison, R. (1976), 'The demoralising experience of prolonged unemployment', *Department of Employment Gazette* (April).

Hart, G. R. (1957), *Retirement: A New Outlook for the Individual* (New York: Harcourt Brace).

Havighurst, R. J. (1954), 'Flexibility and the social roles of the retired', *American Journal Sociology*, vol. 59 (January).

Havighurst, R. J. (1961), 'The nature and values of meaningful free time', in R. T. Kleemeier (ed.), *Aging and Leisure* (London: Oxford University Press).

Havighurst, R. J. (1969), 'Work, leisure and education: toward the goal of creating flexible life styles', *Gerontologist*, vol. 9 (Winter).

Havighurst, R. J., and Albrecht, R. (1953), *Older People* (New York: Longmans, Green).

Havighurst, R. J., and DeVries, A. (1969), 'Life styles and free time activities of retired men', *Human Development*, vol. 12, no. 1.

Havighurst, R. J., Neugarten, B. L., and Tobin, S. S. (1964a), 'Disengagement and patterns of aging', *Gerontologist*, vol. 4 (September).

Havighurst, R. J., Neugarten, B. L., and Tobin, S. S. (1964b), 'Disengagement, personality and life satisfaction in the later years', in P. F. Hansen (ed.), *Age with a Future* (Philadelphia, Penn.: Davis).

Havighurst, R. J., and Shanas, E. (1953), 'Retirement and the professional worker', *Journal of Gerontology*, vol. 8 (January).

Haynes, S. G., McMichael, A. J., and Kupper, L. (1974), 'Mortality around retirement: the rubber industry case', *Gerontologist*, vol. 14 (October).

Haynes, S. G., McMichael, A. J., and Tyroler, H. A. (1977), 'The relationship of normal involuntary retirement to early mortality among US rubber workers', *Social Science and Medicine*, vol. 11, no. 2.

Haynes, S. G., McMichael, A. J., and Tyroler, H. A. (1978), 'Survival after early and normal retirement', *Journal of Gerontology*, vol. 33 (March).

Heidbreder, E. M. (1972), 'Factors in retirement adjustment: white collar/blue collar experience', *Industrial Gerontology*, vol. 12 (Winter).

Help Age International (1977), 'US retirement row' (January).

Heron, A. (1960), 'Ageing and employment', in R. S. Schilling (ed.), *Modern Trends in Occupational Health* (London: Butterworth).

Heron, A. (1962), 'Preparation for retirement: a new phase in occupational development', *Occupational Psychology*, vol. 36 (January and April).

Heron, A., and Chown, S. M. (1963), 'Expectations of supervisors concerning older workers', in R. H. Williams *et al.* (eds), *Processes of Aging* (New York: Atherton Press).

Heyman, D. K., and Jeffers, F. C. (1966), 'Wives and retirement', *Gerontologist*, vol. 6 (March).

Heyman, D. K., and Jeffers, F. C. (1968), 'Wives and retirement: a pilot study', *Journal of Gerontology*, vol. 23 (October).

Hinds, S. W. (1963), 'The personal and socio-medical aspects of retirement', *Royal Society of Health Journal*, vol. 83 (April).

Hoar, J. (1961), 'A study of free time activities of 200 aged persons', *Sociology and Social Research*, vol. 45 (January).

Hochschild, A. R. (1973), *The Unexpected Community* (Englewood Cliffs, NJ: Prentice-Hall).

Hochschild, A. R. (1975), 'Disengagement theory: a critique and proposal', *American Sociological Review*, vol. 40 (October).

Holmberg, A. R. (1961), 'Age in the Andes', in R. W. Kleemeier (ed.), *Aging and Leisure* (New York: Oxford University Press).

Hopper, K., and Guttmacher, S. (1979), 'Rethinking suicide: notes toward a critical epidemiology', *International Journal of Health Services*, vol. 9, no. 3.

Hostetler, J. A. (1974), *Hutterite Society* (Baltimore, Md.: Johns Hopkins University Press).

Howe, A. L. (1980), 'Leisure and the elderly', in D. Mercer and E. Hamilton-Smith (eds), *Recreation Planning and Social Change in Urban Australia* (Malvern, Australia: Sorrett).

Hoyt, G. C. (1954), 'The life of the retired in a trailer park', *American Journal of Sociology*, vol. 59 (January).

Hunt, A. (1978), *The Elderly at Home* (London: HMSO).

Huyck, M. H. (1974), *Growing Older* (Englewood Cliffs, NJ: Prentice-Hall).

International Labour Office (1979), *Older Workers: Work and Retirement* (London: ILO).

International Labor Review (1964), 'Information', vol. 90 (July).

Irelan, L. M., and Bell, D. B. (1972), 'Understanding subjectively defined retirement: a pilot analysis', *Gerontologist*, vol. 12 (Winter).

Iyer, R. N. (1966), 'The social structure of the future', in his *Looking Forward: The Abundant Society* (Santa Barbara, Calif.: Center for the Study of Democratic Institutions).

Jacobson, D. (1971), 'Attitudes towards work and retirement among older industrial workers in three firms' (PhD dissertation, London School of Economics).

Bibliography

Jacobson, D. (1972*a*), 'Fatigue-producing factors in industrial work and pre-retirement attitudes', *Occupational Psychology*, vol. 46.

Jacobson, D. (1972*b*), 'Willingness to retire in relation to job strain and type of work', *Industrial Gerontology*, vol. 13 (Spring).

Jacobson, D. (1974*a*), 'Planning for retirement and anticipatory attitudes towards withdrawal from work', *British Journal of Guidance and Counselling*, vol. 2 (January).

Jacobson, D. (1974*b*), 'Rejection of the retiree role – a study of female industrial workers in their 50s', *Human Relations*, vol. 27, no. 5.

Jaffe, A. J. (1970), 'Men prefer not to retire', *Industrial Gerontology*, vol. 5 (Spring).

Jaffe, A. J. (1972), 'The retirement dilemma', *Industrial Gerontology*, vol. 14 (Summer).

Jaffe, A. J., and Rios, R. J. (1975), 'Retirement and pensions in the republic of Panama', *Industrial Gerontology*, vol. 2 (Summer).

Jarvik, L. F., and Cohen, D. (1973), 'A biobehavioural approach to intellectual changes with aging', in C. Eisdorfer and M. P. Lawton (eds), *The Psychology of Adult Development and Aging* (Washington, DC: American Psychological Association).

Jary, D. (1973), 'Evenings at the ivory tower', in M. A. Smith *et al.* (eds), *Leisure and Society in Britain* (London: Allen Lane).

Jenkins, C., and Sherman, B. (1979), *The Collapse of Work* (London: Eyre, Methuen).

Jenkins, W. (1973), 'Reviewing retirement', in I. Henderson (ed.), *The New Poor* (London: Owen).

Johnson, D. E. (1958), 'A depressive retirement syndrome', *Geriatrics*, vol. 13 (May).

Johnson, G. E. (1951), 'Is a compulsory retirement age ever justified?', *Journal of Gerontology*, vol. 6 (July).

Johnson, J., and Strother, G. B. (1962), 'Job expectations and retirement planning', *Journal of Gerontology*, vol. 17 (October).

Johnston, F. (1955), 'Management and the employment of older workers', in *Report of the Third Congress of the International Association of Gerontology, London 1954* (Edinburgh: Livingstone).

Jonas, D., and D. (1973), *Young till We Die* (London: Hodder & Stoughton).

Jones, A. (1974), 'Work and leisure', in M. Pilch (ed.), *The Retirement Book* (London: Hamish Hamilton).

Jones, R. (1977), *The Other Generation: The New Power of Older People* (Englewood Cliffs, NJ: Prentice-Hall).

Jones, S. (1976), 'The abilities of the elders: theory X and theory Y', in S. Jones (ed.), *Liberation of the the Elders* (London: Beth Johnson Foundation).

Kahn, J. H. (1975), foreword to J. H. Wallis, *Thinking About Retirement* (Oxford: Pergamon).

Kaplan, M. (1979), *Leisure: Lifestyle and Lifespan* (Philadelphia, Penn.: Saunders)

Karn, V. (1974), *Retiring to the Seaside* (London: Age Concern).

Kasschau, P. L. (1976), 'Retirement and the social system', *Industrial Gerontology*, vol. 3 (Winter).

Kemp, F., and Buttle, B. (1979), *Focus on Retirement* (London: Kogan Page).

Kent, D. (1965), 'Aging: fact and fancy', *Gerontologist*, vol. 5 (March).

Kerckhoff, A. C. (1964), 'Husband–wife expectations and reactions to retirement', *Journal of Gerontology*, vol. 19 (October).

Kimmel, D. C., Price, K. F., and Walker, J. W. (1978), 'Retirement choice and retirement satisfaction', *Journal of Gerontology*, vol. 33 (July).

Kleemeier, R. W. (1951), 'The effect of a work program on adjustment attitudes in an aged population', *Journal of Gerontology*, vol. 6 (October).

Kleemeier, R. W. (1964), 'Leisure and disengagement in retirement', *Gerontologist*, vol. 4 (December).

Knapp, M. R. (1977), 'Activity theory of aging: an examination in the English context', *Gerontologist*, vol. 17 (December).

Koller, M. R. (1968), *Social Gerontology* (New York: Random House).

Kooy, G. A., Van't Klooster, and Van Wingerden, C. M. (1968), 'The aged in an urban community in the Netherlands', *Human Development*, vol. 11, no. 1.

Kratcoski, P. C., Huber, J. H., and Gaulak, R. (1974), 'Retirement satisfaction among emeritus professors', *Industrial Gerontology*, vol. 1 (Winter).

Lawton, M. P. (1978), 'Leisure activities for the aged', *Annals of the American Academy of Political and Social Science*, vol. 438 (July).

Lefkowitz, B. (1979), *Break Time* (New York: Hawthorn Books).

Lehman, H. C. (1953), *Age and Achievement* (Princeton, NJ: Princeton University Press).

Lehman, H. C. (1955), 'Jobs for those over sixty-five', *Journal of Gerontology*, vol. 10 (July).

Lehr, U. and Dreher, G. (1969), 'Determinants of attitudes toward retirement', in R. J. Havighurst *et al.* (eds), *Adjustment to Retirement* (Assen: Van Gorcum).

Lemon, B. W., Bengston, V. L., and Peterson, J. A. (1972), 'An exploration of the activity theory of aging', *Journal of Gerontology*, vol. 27 (October).

Lipman, A. (1964), 'Loss of status in retirement', *Gerontologist*, vol. 4 (September).

Lipman, A., and Smith, K. J. (1968), 'Functionality of disengagement in old age', *Journal of Gerontology*, vol. 23 (October).

Lishman, G. (1975), *A Redefinition of Retirement* (London: Liberal Publication Department).

Liu, Y. (1974), 'Retirees and retirement programs in the People's Republic of China', *Industrial Gerontology*, vol. 1 (Spring).

Livson, F. (1962), 'Adjustment to retirement', in S. Reichard *et al.* (eds), *Aging and Personality* (New York: Wiley).

Loether, H. J. (1964), 'The meaning of work and adjustment to retirement', in A. B. Shostak and W. Gomberg (eds), *Blue Collar World* (Englewood Cliffs, NJ: Prentice-Hall).

Loether, H. J. (1975), *Problems of Aging: Sociological and Social Psychological Perspectives*, 2nd edn (Encino, Calif: Dickenson).

Logan, W. F. D. (1953), 'Work and age: statistical considerations', *British Medical Journal*, vol. 28 (November).

Loudoun, Countess of (1977), debate on 'The problems of retirement', House of Lords, *Hansard*, vol. 379 (2 February), col. 23.

Bibliography

Lowenthal, M. F. (1964), 'Social isolation and mental illness in old age', *American Sociological Review*, vol. 29 (January).

Lowenthal, M. F. (1966), 'Perspectives for leisure and retirement', in R. Brockbank and D. Westerby-Gibson (eds), *Mental Health in a Changing Community* (New York: Grune & Stratton).

Lowenthal, M. F., Berkman, P. L., and associates (1967), *Aging and Mental Disorder in San Francisco* (San Francisco; New York: Jossey-Bass).

McGoldrick, A., and Cooper, C. L. (1980), 'Voluntary early retirement – taking the decision', *Employment Gazette* (August).

Maddox, G. L. (1963), 'Activity and morale: a longitudinal study of elderly subjects', *Social Forces*, vol. 42.

Maddox, G. L. (1964), 'Disengagement theory: a critical evaluation', *Gerontologist*, vol. 4 (June).

Maddox, G. L. (1965), 'Fact and artifact: evidence bearing on disengagement theory from the Duke Geriatrics Project', *Human Development*, vol. 8, no. 1.

Maddox, G. L. (1966), 'Retirement as a social event in the United States', in T. C. McKinney and F. T. de Vyver (eds), *Aging and Social Policy* (New York: Appleton-Century-Crofts).

Maddox, G. L. (1968), 'Retirement as a social event', in B. L. Neugarten (ed.), *Middle Age and Aging* (Chicago: Chicago University Press).

Manard, B. B. (1975), *Old-Age Institutions* (Lexington, Mass.: D. C. Heath (Lexington Books)).

Martin, J., and Doran, A. (1966), 'Evidence concerning the relationship between health and retirement', *Sociological Review*, vol. 14 (November).

Meier, E. L. (1975), 'Over 65: explanations and realities of work and retirement', *Industrial Gerontology*, vol. 2 (Spring).

Meier, E. L., and Kerr, E. (1976), 'Capabilities of middle-aged and older workers: a survey of the literature', *Industrial Gerontology*, vol. 3 (Summer).

Miller, H. (1978), *Countdown to Retirement* (London: Hutchinson).

Miller, H. C. (1963), *The Ageing Countryman* (London: National Corporation for the Care of Old People).

Ministry of Pensions and National Insurance Report (1954), *Reasons Given for Retiring or Continuing at Work* (London: HMSO).

Mitchell, W. M. (1972), 'Lay observations on retirement', in F. M. Carp (ed.), *Retirement* (New York: Behavioural Publications).

Moore, E. H., and Streib, G. F. (1959), *The Nature of Retirement* (New York: Macmillan).

Morrison, M. H. (1975), 'The myth of employee planning for retirement', *Industrial Gerontology*, vol. 2 (Spring).

Morrison, M. H. (1979), 'International developments in retirement flexibility', *Aging and Work*, vol. 2 (Fall).

Mossman, K. (1971), *Looking Forward to Retirement* (London: Ward Lock).

Motley, D. K. (1978), 'Availability of retired persons for work: findings from the Retirement History study', *Social Security Bulletin*, vol. 41 (April).

Myers, R. J. (1954), 'Factors in interpreting mortality after retirement', *Journal of the American Statistical Association*, vol. 49 (September).

Nahemow, N., and Adams, B. N. (1974), 'Old age among the Baganda:

continuity and change', in J. F. Gubrium (ed.), *Late Life: Communities and Environmental Policy* (Springfield, Ill.: C. C. Thomas).

National Advisory Committee on the Employment of Older Men and Women (1953), *First Report* (1955), *Second Report* (London: HMSO).

Neugarten, B. L. (1969), 'Disengagement reconsidered in a cross-national context', in R. J. Havighurst *et al.* (eds), *Adjustment to Retirement* (Assen: Van Gorcum).

Niemi, T. (1980), 'Retirement and mortality', *Scandinavian Journal of Social Medicine*, vol. 8, no. 1.

Norris, A. H., and Shock, N. W. (1955), 'Age differences in the efficiency of manual exercise in males', in *Report of the Third Congress of the International Association of Gerontology, London 1954* (Edinburgh: Livingstone).

Odell, C. (1959), 'Employment and pre-retirement problems of the older worker', *Geriatrics*, vol. 14, pt I, 'Productivity of the older worker' (July); pt III, 'Retirement preparation education' (September); pt IV, 'Phased retirement' (October).

Office of Population Censuses and Surveys (OPCS) (1978), *Demographic Review, 1977* (London: OPCS).

Oldfield, M. H. (1968), 'Part-time work', in H. B. Wright (ed.), *Solving the Problems of Retirement* (London: Institute of Directors).

Olsen, H., and Hansen, G. (1977), *Retirement from Work* (Copenhagen: Danish Institute of Social Research).

Organisation for European Co-operation and Development (OECD) (1971), *Adaptation and Employment of Special Groups of Manpower – Policies on Age and Employment* (Paris: OECD).

Organisation for European Co-operation and Development (OECD) (1973), *New Patterns for Working Time* (Paris: OECD).

Owen, J. P., and Belzung, L. D. (1967), 'Consequences of voluntary early retirement', *British Journal of Industrial Relations*, vol. 5 (July).

Palmore, E. G. (1965), 'Differences in the retirement patterns of men and women', *Gerontologist*, vol. 5 (March).

Palmore, E. G. (1969), 'Physical, mental and social factors in predicting longevity', *Gerontologist*, vol. 9.

Palmore, E. G. (1971), 'Why do people retire?', *Aging and Human Development*, vol. 2 (November).

Palmore, E. G. (1972), 'Compulsory versus flexible retirement: issues and facts', *Gerontologist*, vol. 12 (Winter).

Palmore, E. G. (1975), *The Honorable Elders* (Durham, NC: Duke University Press).

Parker, S. (1972), *The Future of Work and Leisure* (London: Paladin).

Parker, S. (1980), *Older Workers and Retirement* (London: HMSO).

Parker, S., Brown, R., Child, J., and Smith, M. (1981), *The Sociology of Industry*, 4th edn (London: Allen & Unwin).

Parran, T., *et al.* (1953), 'Retirement of older workers', in G. Mathiason (ed.), *Criteria for Retirement* (New York: Putnam).

Pasterfield, D. (1981), 'The do-it-yourself road to retirement', *Pre-Retirement Choice* (January).

Bibliography

Peppers, L. F. (1976), 'Patterns of leisure and adjustment to retirement', *Gerontologist*, vol. 16 (October).

Peretti, P. O., and Wilson, C. (1975), 'Voluntary and involuntary retirement of aged males and their effect on emotional satisfaction, usefulness, self-image, emotional stability, and interpersonal relationships', *Aging and Human Development*, vol. 6, no. 2.

Phillipson, C. (1978), 'The emergence of retirement', Working Papers in Sociology, no. 14 (Durham: Durham University Press).

Pollak, O. (1948), *Social Adjustment in Old Age* (New York: Social Science Research Council).

Prasad, B. S. (1964), 'The retirement postulate of the disengagement theory', *Gerontologist*, vol. 4 (March).

Prentis, R. S. (1980), 'White-collar working women's perception of retirement', *Gerontologist*, vol. 20 (February).

Pre-Retirement Choice (1976), 'Forging links for old skills' (August).

Pre-Retirement Choice (1975), 'Weighted pensions' (March).

Price, K. F., Walker, J. W., and Kimmel, D. C. (1979), 'Retirement timing and retirement satisfaction', *Aging and Work*, vol. 2 (Fall).

Pyke, M. (1980), *Long Life* (London: Dent).

Pyron, H. C., and Manion, U. V. (1973), 'Preretirement counseling', in J. G. Cull and R. E. Hardy (eds), *The Neglected Older American* (Springfield, Ill.: C. C. Thomas).

Queen, S. A., and Gruener, J. R. (1940), *Social Pathology: Obstacles to Social Participation* (New York: Crowell).

Rainsbury, J. P. (1970), 'Retirement preparation schemes: experience at Rubery Owen', *Gerontology*, vol. 1 (April).

Rapoport, R., Rapoport, R. N., and Strelitz, J. (1977), *Fathers, Mothers and Others* (London: Routledge & Kegan Paul).

Reichard, S., Livson, F., and Peterson, P. G. (1968), 'Adjustment to retirement', in B. L. Neugarten, ed., *Middle Age and Aging* (Chicago: Chicago University Press).

Reno, V. (1971), 'Why men stop working at or before age 65', *Social Security Bulletin*, vol. 34 (June).

Rhee, H. A. (1974), *Human Ageing and Retirement* (Geneva: International Social Security Association).

Richardson, I. M. (1956), 'Retirement: a social-medical study of 244 men', *Scottish Medical Journal*, vol. 1 (December).

Riesman, D. (1954), 'Some clinical and cultural aspects of the ageing process', *American Journal of Sociology*, vol. 59 (January).

Riffault, H. (1978), *The Attitude of the Working Population to Retirement* (Brussels: Commission of the European Communities).

Riley, M. W., and Foner, A. (1968), *Aging and Society*, Vol. 1: *An Inventory of Research Findings* (New York: Russell Sage).

Roman, P., and Taietz, P. (1967), 'Organizational structure and disengagement: the emeritus professor', *Gerontologist*, vol. 7 (September).

Rose, A. M. (1964), 'A current theoretical issue in social gerontology', *Gerontologist*, vol. 4 (March).

Rose, A. M. (1965), 'Group consciousness among the aging', in A. M. Rose and W. A. Peterson (eds), *Older People and their Social World* (Oxford: Blackwell).

Rose, C. L. (1964), 'Social factors in longevity', *Gerontologist*, vol. 4 (March).

Rose, C. L. (1974), 'Preferred age of retirement: a casual analysis', paper presented to Gerontological Society 27th Annual Scientific Meeting, Portland, Oregon.

Rose, C. L., and Mogey, J. M. (1972), 'Aging and preference for later retirement', *Aging and Human Development*, vol. 3 (February).

Rosenfeld, C., and Waldman, E. (1967), 'Work limitations and chronic health problems', *Monthly Labor Review*, vol. 92 (January).

Rosow, I. (1967), *Social Integration of the Aged* (Glencoe, Ill.: Free Press).

Rosow, I. (1974), *Socialization to Old Age* (Berkeley, Calif.: University of California Press).

Rowland, R. H. (1975), 'Withdrawal from the work force among persons of retirement age in the USSR, 1959–1970', *Industrial Geronotology*, vol. 2 (Spring).

Rustom, C. (1961), 'The later years of life and the use of time among the Burmans', in R. W. Kleemeier (ed.), *Aging and Leisure* (New York: Oxford University Press).

Rynne, C. (1973), *Enjoying Retirement* (Dublin: Tore Books).

Saleh, S. D. (1964), 'A study of attitude change in the pre-retirement period', *Journal of Applied Psychology*, vol. 48 (October).

Saleh, S. D., and Otis, J. L. (1963), 'Sources of job satisfaction and their effects on attitudes toward retirement', *Journal of Industrial Psychology*, vol. 1.

Samson, E. (1972), *Future Perfect: Retirement Planning and Management* (London: Kimpton).

Sauvy, A. (1948), 'Social and economic consequences of the ageing of Western European populations', *Population Studies* (June).

Schwab, K. (1974), 'Early labor-force withdrawal of men: participants and nonparticipants aged 58–63', *Social Security Bulletin*, vol. 37 (August).

Shanas, E. (1958), 'Facts versus stereotypes: the Cornell Study of Occupational Retirement', *Journal of Social Issues*, vol. 14, no. 2.

Shanas, E. (1972), 'Adjustment to retirement: substitution or accommodation?', in F. Carp (ed.), *Retirement* (New York: Behavioural Publications).

Shanas, E., Townsend, P., Wedderburn, D., Friis, H., Milhj, P., and Stehouwer, J. (eds) (1968), *Old People in Three Industrial Societies* (London: Routledge & Kegan Paul).

Shenfield, B. E. (1955), 'Employment prospects for older workers in Great Britain', in *Report of the Third Congress of the International Association of Gerontology, London 1954* (Edinburgh: Livingstone).

Shenfield, B. E. (1957), *Social Policies for Old Age* (London: Routledge & Kegan Paul).

Sheppard, H. L. (1978), 'The issue of mandatory retirement', *Annals of the American Academy of Political and Social Science*, vol. 438 (July).

Sheppard, H. L., and Rix, S. E. (1977), *The Graying of Working America: the Coming Crisis in Retirement-age Policy* (New York: Free Press).

Showler, B. (1977), 'Employment and the older worker', *Age Concern Today* (Spring).

Bibliography

Simmons, L. W. (1945), *The Role of the Aged in Primitive Society* (New Haven, Conn.: Yale University Press).

Simon, A. W. (1968), *The New Years* (London: Gollancz).

Simpson, I. H., Back, K. W., and McKinney (eds) (1966), *Social Aspects of Aging* (Durham, NC: Duke University Press).

Skoglund, J. (1979), 'Work after retirement', *Aging and Work*, vol. 2 (Spring).

Slavick, F., Smith, P. C., Shultz, E. B. and McConnell, J. W. (1962), 'Scope, goals and methodology for a study of retirement policies and practices in the American economy', in C. Tibbitts and W. Donahue (eds), *Social and Psychological Aspects of Aging* (New York: Columbia Press).

Smith, C. M. (1974), *Retirement: The Organisation and the Individual* (London: British Institute of Management).

Smith, M. W. (1953), 'Older workers' efficiency in jobs of various types', *Personnel Journal*, vol. 32 (May).

Smith, R. F. W. (1957), 'Education for a lifetime', *Journal of Educational Sociology*, vol. 30 (January).

Snow, R. B., and Havighurst, R. J. (1977), 'Life style types and patterns of retirement of educators, *Gerontology*, vol. 17 (December).

Spence, D. L. (1968), 'Patterns of retirement in San Francisco', in F. M. Carp (ed.), *The Retirement Process* (Washington, DC: US Government Printing Office).

Stagner, R. (1971), 'An industrial psychologist looks at industrial gerontology', *Aging and Human Development*, vol. 2 (February).

Stagner, R. (1978), 'The affluent society versus early retirement', *Aging and Work*, vol. 1 (Summer).

Stearns, P. N. (1977), *Old Age in European Society* (London: Croom Helm).

Stecker, M. L. (1951), 'Beneficiaries prefer to work', *Social Security Bulletin*, vol. 14 (January).

Streib, G. F. (1956), 'Morale of the retired', *Social Problems*, vol. 3 (April).

Streib, G. F. (1968), 'Disengagement theory in socio-cultural perspective', *International Journal of Psychiatry*, vol. 6 (July).

Sussman, M. B. (1972), 'An analytical model for the sociological study of retirement', in F. M. Carp (ed.), *Retirement* (New York: Behavioural Publications).

Szalai, A. (1976), 'The future of free time', *Futures*, vol. 8 (June).

Szewczuk, W. (1966), 'Rehabilitation of the aged by means of new forms of activity', *Gerontologist*, vol. 6 (December).

Tallmer, M. (1967), 'Social, economic and health factors in disengagement in the aging' (Phd dissertation, Yeshiva University).

Tallmer, M., and Kutner, B. (1969), 'Disengagement and the stresses of aging', *Journal of Gerontology*, vol. 24 (January).

Talmon, Y. (1961), 'Aging in Israel, a planned society', *American Journal of Sociology*, vol. 67 (November).

Taves, M. J., and Hansen, G. D. (1963), 'Seventeen hundred elderly citizens', in A. M. Rose (ed.), *Aging in Minnesota* (Minneapolis, Minn.: Minnesota University Press).

Taylor, C. (1972), 'Developmental conceptions and the retirement process', in F. M. Carp (ed), *Retirement* (New York: Behavioural Publications).

193

Taylor, R. (1976), 'Male retirement', *New Society* (26 August).

Thane, P. (1978), 'The muddled history of retiring at 60 and 65', *New Society* (3 August).

Thompson, G. B. (1973), 'Work versus leisure roles: an investigation of morale among employed and retired men', *Journal of Gerontology*, vol. 28 (July).

Thompson, W. E., and Streib, G. F. (1958), 'Situational determinants: health and economic deprivation in retirement', *Journal of Social Issues*, vol. 14, no. 2.

Thompson, W. E., Streib, G. F., and Kosa, J. (1960), 'The effect of retirement on personal adjustment', *Journal of Gerontology*, vol. 15 (April).

Tibbitts, C. (1954), 'Retirement problems in American society', *American Journal of Sociology*, vol. 59 (January).

Titmuss, R. M. (1968), *Commitment to Welfare* (London: Allen & Unwin).

Tinker, A. (1981), *The Elderly in Modern Society* (London: Longman).

Townsend, P. (1957), *The Family Life of Old People* (London: Routledge & Kegan Paul).

Tracy, M. B. (1978), 'Flexible retirement features abroad', *Social Security Bulletin*, vol. 41 (May).

Tracy, M. (1979), *Retirement Age Practices in Ten Industrial Societies, 1960–1976* (Geneva: International Social Security Association).

Tunstall, J. (1966), *Old and Alone* (London: Routledge & Kegan Paul).

Tyhurst, J. S., Salk, L., and Kennedy, M. (1957), 'Mortality, morbidity, and retirement', *American Journal of Public Health*, vol. 47 (November).

Vickery, K. O. A. (1969), 'Post retirement and later days', *Royal Society of Health Journal*, vol. 89 (July).

Walker, A. (1980), 'The social creation of poverty and dependency in old age', *Journal of Social Policy*, vol. 9 (January).

Walker, J. W., and Lazer, H. L. (1978), *The End of Mandatory Retirement* (New York: Wiley).

Weiss, E. J. (1978), *The Best Is Yet to Be . . . ?* (Portland, Oreg.: Oregon Bureau of Labor).

Welford, A. T. (1958), *Ageing and Human Skill* (London: Oxford University Press).

Whitehead, T. (1978), 'Ageing and the mind', in D. Hobman (ed.), *The Social Challenge of Ageing* (London: Croom Helm).

Withers, W. (1974), 'Some irrational beliefs about retirement in the United States', *Industrial Gerontology*, vol. 1 (Winter).

Wolfbein, S. L. (1963), 'Changing patterns of working life', *Monthly Labor Review*, vol. 88 (August).

Wolff, K. (1959), *The Biological, Sociological and Psychological Aspects of Aging* (Springfield, Ill.: C. C. Thomas).

Wood, V., and Bultena, G. (1969), 'The American retirement community: bane or blessing?', *Journal of Gerontology*, vol. 24 (April).

Wright, H. B. (1975), *Executive Ease and Dis-ease* (Epping, Essex: Gower Press).

Zborowski, M. (1962), 'Aging and recreation', *Journal of Gerontology*, vol. 17 (July).

Zborowski, M., and Herzog, E. (1952), *Life Is with People* (New York: Schocken Books).

Index

Index

Names in the text are indexed, but names in the bibliography are not

Aberdeen 94
Abkhasia people 28
Abrams, A. J. 165
Abrams, M. 21-2, 127
absenteeism 85
accommodation theory 61
Achenbaum, A. 20
activity theory 13, 38, 51, 58-60, 63
Acuff, G. 132
Adams, D. 29, 180
Africa 29
Age Concern 67, 75, 78, 133, 157, 167
ageing 14, 42-3, 53ff, 79ff, 104, 139, 153
ageism 15, 24
Aiken, L. 167
Albrecht, R. 157
Allen, D. 132
Anderson, B. 115
Anderson, J. E. 100
Anderson, W. F. 65, 69, 70, 94
Andes peasants 28
Ash, P. 65
Atchley, R. C. 25, 32, 34, 44, 53, 58, 61, 62, 101, 139
Atkinson, A. M. 72
Australia 74

Back, K. W. 33, 79
Baganda people 29
Barr, P. 157
Barrett, J. H. 41
Barron, M. L. 151
barter 14, 128, 137
Bauder, W. W. 26
Baulch, N. 144
Baum, M. and R. C. 61
Beethoven 174
Belbin, R. M. 19, 37, 40, 83
Belgium 162

Bell, D. B. 33
Belzung, L. D. 90
Bengston, V. L. 126, 132
Berglind, H. 92
Best, F. 160, 163
Beveridge Report 18
Beveridge, W. E. 25, 59, 77, 99, 102-3
bingo 172, 174
Bixby, L. 33
Blaire, T. 128
Blaxter, M. 101
Bonn 54
boredom 104, 109, 116, 130, 142
Boston 69
Bratthall, K. 162
Breckinridge, E. L. 85
Breen, L. Z. 25
Brehm, H. P. 55
Bristol 112
Brown, J. C. 177
Brown, R. G. 82
building industry 86
Bultena, G. 147
Burma 29
Butler, R. N. 112
Buttle, B. 73

Cain, L. 38
California 60, 100
Canada 119, 124, 177
Cameron, N. 113
Cannon, L. 160
Caro, F. 101, 131, 145
Carp, F. 34
Cesa-Bianchi, M. 38
Chicago 36, 54, 132
China 28
Ciribosa, D. A. 126, 132
Chown, S. M. 84, 157
Christ, E. A. 146
Christrup, H. 76

Cicero 88
Citizen's Advice Bureaux 78
civil servants 16, 89
Clark, F. le Gros 37, 86, 125
Clark, M. 27, 65, 115
class, social 117 (*see also* socio-economic status)
Cohen, D. 83
Cole, S. 85
Comfort, A. 21
compromise/negotiation theory 62
continuity theory 61
Cooley, L. F. and L. M. 88
Cooper, C. L. 90
Cornell Study of Occupational Retirement 79
Corson, J. H. 96-8
Council of Europe 133
Cowan, N. R. 94
Cowgill, D. O. 57, 144
Crawford, M. P. 56, 78, 112
Cumming, E. M. 52, 55-8
Cunningham, D. A. 139

Daniel, W. W. 92
Daric, J. 85
day centres 47, 50
day-release 73
de Beauvoir, S. 143
DeJong, G. F. 76
Denmark 104, 133
Dennis, W. 85
Department of Health and Social Security 165
Desai, K. G. 128
DeVries, A. 54
disengagement theory 13, 31, 38, 40, 44, 63, 51-8, 63
Doerflinger, J. F. 26
do-it-yourself 127, 137
Donovan and Associates Pty Ltd 74
Doran, A. 111
Draper, J. E. 100
Dreher, G. 53, 68
Duke University Geriatrics Project 55
Dumazedier, J. 174

Dunbar, J. 155
Dunne, A. C. 125

education 13-14, 29, 73-4, 77, 102, 117, 129, 162-5, 170-4, 178-9
Eisdorfer, C. 169
Emerson, A. R. 144
employers 11, 36, 73ff, 87, 92-4, 99, 103, 124, 134-7, 159, 168, 174
employment 14, 22, 26, 32, 46, 48, 70-1, 82ff, 102-3, 113ff, 123ff, 163ff (*see also* work)
engineering 18, 75
Epstein, L. A. 126
Estes, C. L. 53
Evans, W. 33

farmers 28
Fengler, A. P. 121
Fillenbaum, G. G. 70, 76, 126
Finland 119
Fischer, D. H. 20
fishermen 28
Fleming, C. E. 71
flexibility 41, 44, 104
flexible life styles 15, 150, 162-5, 172, 178
Florida 48
Fogarty, M. 88, 177
Foner, A. 26
foster grandparents 129, 167
Fox, A. J. 119
Fox, J. H. 40
freedom 102, 105
France 53, 85, 124, 133, 162
Fried, E. G. 131
Friedmann, E. A. 99, 114, 143
functional(ist) theory 53, 57, 62-3, 178

Gaulak, R. 131
Geist, H. 113
General Household Survey 117
George, L. K. 116
Germany 124, 157, 162
Ginzberg, E. 70
Glamser, F. D. 76

Glasgow 73, 94
Glenn, N. D. 83
Gordon, M. S. 95
Gore, I. 164
Goudy, W. J. 69
Goyder, C. 164
Gray Panthers 176
Greece 92
Griffiths, T. 75
Groombridge, B. 171
Gruener, J. R. 57
Gubrium, J. F. 129
Guttmacher, S. 120

Hall, H. 69
Hansen, G. D. 101, 131, 133-4, 145, 158
Harris, A. 144
Hart, G. R. 118
Havighurst, R. J. 37, 41, 42, 54, 58, 82, 114, 157, 163
Haynes, S. G. 68, 119
health, as reason for retirement 90-1, 94-8, 107
Heidbreder, E. M. 90
Help Age International 150
Help the Aged 78
Henry, W. 52, 55-8
Hepworth and Grandage 75
Herma, J. 70
Heron, A. 84, 157
Herzog, E. 27
Heyman, D. K. 120
Hinds, S. W. 32, 38
Hoar, J. 147
Hochschild, A. R. 55, 143
Holmberg, A. R. 28
Hopper, K. 120
Hostetler, J. A. 28
housewives 40
housing 118
Howe, A. L. 39
Hoyt, G. C. 100
Huber, J. H. 131
Hunt, A. 65, 95, 97
Hutterites 27
Huyck, M. H. 62

identity, occupational 103, 115
income 21, 24, 46, 91ff, 103-4, 108, 115-8, 153 (*see also* money)
industrial workers 54, 66-7, 71, 102, 150, 157
industrialisation 26
Institute for Retired Professionals 129
interaction, social 58-9
International Labor Review 92
International Labour Office 123, 162
Irelan, L. M. 33
Ireland 53
Israel 28
Italy 124
Iyer, R. N. 163

Jacobson, D. 66, 67, 112, 150, 157
Jaffe, A. J. 29, 82, 95-6, 98, 125, 167
Japan, 28, 126, 162
Jarvik, L. F. 83
Jary, D. 171
Jeffers, F. C. 120
Jenkins, C. 173
Jenkins, W. 166
job-sharing 168-9
Johnson, D. E. 112
Johnson, G. E. 70
Johnston, F. 84
Jonas, D. and D. 167
Jones, A. 102
Jones, R. 28, 136, 162
Jones, S. 88

Kahn, J. H. 148
Kansas City 53, 58
Kaplan, M. 32
Karn, V. 133
Kasschau, P. L. 34
Keith, P. 69
Keller, A. B. 126, 132, 139
Kemp, F. 73
Kennedy, M. 119
Kent, D. 77
Kerckhoff, A. C. 99
Kerr, E. 87
Kimmel, D. C. 79, 99

199

Kleemeier, R. W. 58, 136
Knapp, M. R. 60
Koller, M. R. 29
Kooy, G. A. 144
Kosa, J. 36
Kratcoski, P. C. 131
Kupper, L. 68
Kutner, B. 56

Lawton, M. P. 147
lawyers 167
Lazer, H. L. 151
Lefkowitz, B. 164
Lehman, H. C. 86, 126
Lehr, U. 53, 68
leisure 14, 22ff, 32, 47, 60, 69, 91, 96,
    105-6, 116-17, 133, 138-49,
    162ff
Lemon, B. W. 60
linear lifestyles 15, 163, 172, 178
Link Opportunity 128
Lipman, A. 54, 117
Lishman, G. 166
Liu, Y. 28
Livson, F. 43, 100
Loether, H. J. 41, 101
Logan, W. F. D. 82
London 102
loneliness 48, 80, 116
longevity 20, 118, 136
Los Angeles 101
Loudoun, Countess of 166
Lowenthal, M. F. 40, 112
lumbermen 28
Lundgren, E. F. 100

McConnell, J. W. 96-8
McGoldrick, A. 90
McKeown, T. 82
McKinney, J. C. 79
McMichael, A. J. 68, 119
Maddox, G. L. 41, 55, 56, 59, 126
managers 44, 59, 71, 74, 84, 100, 117,
    127, 141, 160
Manard, B. B. 126
Manion, U. V. 77
Martin, J. 111

Meier, E. L. 87, 150
memory 83
Metzner, H. L. 139
Milan 39, 54
Miller, H. 73
Miller, H. C. 117
mining 18
Ministry of Pensions and National
    Insurance 93, 97
Minnesota 157
Mitchell, W. M. 33, 42
mobility, occupational 169
Mogey, J. M. 69
money 24, 68, 71-2, 103, 108, 130
Montoye, H. J. 139
Moore, E. H. 31, 38
Morrison, M. H. 79, 124
Mossman, K. 73
Motley, D. K. 134
Murray, J. H. 126
Murray, Len 176
Myers, J. 119

Nahemow, N. 29
Naik, R. D. I. 28
Nation's Business 158
National Advisory Committee on the
    Employment of Older Men and
    Women 130, 165
Netherlands 124, 144
Neugarten, B. L. 58
neuroses 83
New School for Social Research 129
New York 129, 136
Niemi, T. 119
Nijmegen 54
Norris, A. H. 84
North Carolina 120
Northcote-Trevelyan Report 16
Norway 162
Nyakusa people 29

Odell, C. 161
Office of Population Censuses and
    Surveys 11
Old People's Welfare Associations 78
Oldfield, M. H. 166

Olsen, H. 133
Orbach, H. L. 99
Oregon University 90
Organisation for European Co-operation and Development 157, 164
Otis, J. L. 69
Owen, J. P. 90

Palmore, E. G. 28, 33, 96, 126, 136, 151
Panama 29
Parker, S. 22, 32-3, 67, 70ff, 91ff, 104-10, 124ff, 140, 144-5, 155, 160
Parran, T. 96-8
Pasterfield, D. 78
pensions 11ff, 29ff, 46, 89, 92, 121, 158ff, 170, 175
Peppers, L. F. 100, 139
Peretti, P. O. 36
Peterson, P. G. 43
Phillipson, C. 19
policemen 17
policies 11, 24, 80, 150-79
    early retirement 92
    employment 13, 81, 137, 170, 175
    leisure 174
    retirement 12, 15, 34, 37, 44, 63, 87, 124, 144, 151, 177-8
Pollak, O. 39
Portland 158
Powers, E. A. 69
Prasad, B. S. 54
Prentis, R. S. 75
Pre-Retirement Association 78
Pre-Retirement Choice 128, 156
pre-retirement courses 78, 180
Price, K. F. 79, 99
productivity 83-6
professional occupations 37, 71, 85, 117, 127, 131, 165
psychoses 83
Pyke, M. 172
Pyron, H. C. 77

quality of life 162
Queen, S. A. 57

railway companies 17

Raisbury, J. P. 75
Rapoport, R. and R. N. 120
recreation 174
redundancies 35, 95, 101, 134
Reichard, S. 43
Reno, V. 91
retirement
    adjustment to 41-3, 61, 76, 79, 98-101, 146, 152
    administrative 91, 98, 121
    age of 28-9, 35, 89
    attitudes to 36-7, 40-4, 66-73
    communities 129, 147
    conceptual approaches 34-5
    councils 78
    counselling 77, 170
    decisions 34-5, 63, 151
    definitions 31-3
    early 19ff, 35, 79, 89-93, 98, 156, 177
    experience of 11, 14, 44-52, 89-122
    flexible 15, 157-60
    future of 175-7
    gains in 102-3, 121
    gradual 15, 21, 27ff, 157, 160-2
    health in 56, 107, 110-14, 153, 166
    history of 12, 16-20
    in agricultural societies 26
    losses in 103-4, 121
    meaning of 104-10
    migration 11
    morale in 54-5, 113-18
    mortality in 118-20
    myth of 138-9
    norms for 25
    phases of 38-9, 44
    preparation for 13, 15, 36, 64-80, 140-3, 170, 178
    problems of 68
    prospect of 66-8
    reasons for 93-8
    satisfaction in 40, 99
    settling down in 99
    types 35-7
    voluntary 35-6, 90, 94-6, 150-6, 162

retirement (*cont.*)
wives' attitudes to husbands' 102, 116, 120-1
Retirement History Study 91, 96-7, 134
Rhee, H. A. 40, 58
Richardson, I. M. 94
Riesman, D. 42, 52
Riffault, H. 130
Riley, M. W. 26
Rios, R. J. 29
Ripert, A. 174
Rix, S. E. 158, 176
Roman, P. 57
Rose, A. M. 54-5
Rose, C. L. 68-9, 136
Rosenfeld, C.
Rosow, I. 25, 145
Rowland, R. H. 27
Rubery Owen 75
Russell Report 74
Rustom, C. 29
Rynne, C. 132

sabbaticals 164, 173
Saleh, S. D. 69
Salk, L. 119
Samson, E. 102, 143
San Francisco 112, 115
Sauvy, A. 118
Schwab, K. 91
self-employment 26, 126, 161
Shanas, E. 37, 61, 79, 104, 111, 134
Sheffield 71
sheltered workshops 167
Shenfield, B. E. 135, 166
Sheppard, H. L. 155, 158, 176
Sherman, B. 173
Shock, N. W. 84
Showler, B. 24
Simmons, L. W. 27
Simpson, I. H. 79
Skoglund, J. 133
Slavick, F. 151
Smith, C. M. 74, 160
Smith, K. J. 54
Smith, M. W. 84

Smith, R. F. W. 171
Snow, R. B. 42
socio-economic status 42, 45, 64, 70-1, 99, 120, 127, 131
Soviet Union 27, 175
Spence, D. L. 112
Stagner, R. 86, 169
Stearns, P. N. 132
Stecker, M. L. 131
steelworkers 54, 65
Streib, G. F. 31, 36, 38, 53, 111ff
Strelitz, Z. 120
Strother, G. B. 70, 100
substitution theory 61
suicide 119-20
Sweden 124, 133, 162
Switzerland 133
Szalai, A. 135
Szewczuk, W. 59

Taietz, P. 57
Tallmer, M. 56
Talmon, Y. 28
Taves, M. J. 101, 131, 145, 158
Taylor, C. 72
Taylor, R. 175
teachers 17, 54, 167
technology 22, 166, 179
Texas 90
textiles 18
Thane, P. 17
Thompson, G. B. 113
Thompson, W. E. 36, 111, 119
Thurman, C. 76
Tinker, A. 125
Titmuss, R. M. 16
Tobin, S. S. 58
Townsend, P. 167
Tracy, M. B. 92, 162
trade unions 17, 18, 22, 24, 45, 73, 152, 169
transport 118
Tunstall, J. 116
Tyhurst, J. S. 119
Tyroler, H. A. 119

unemployment 18, 19, 35, 87, 93, 101, 115, 133, 135, 175

Index

USA 16, 20, 24, 27, 33, 38, 42, 65, 68, 76, 79, 82, 85, 89ff, 104, 111, 120, 124ff, 143-4, 150, 155ff, 170, 176

Van't Klooster 144
Van Wingerden 144
Vickery, K. U. A. 17
Vienna 54

Waldman, E. 82
Walker, A. 38, 79
Walker, J. W. 99, 151
Warsaw 54
Washington 76
Weiss, E. J. 158
Welford, A. T. 82
Whitehead, T. 78
Whitfield, A. G. W. 82
Wilson, C.
Wisconsin 100
Withers, W. 24
Wolfbein, S. L. 116
Wolff, R. 115

Wood, V. 146
work
  after retirement age 14
  and leisure 14, 140-2, 149
  capacities for 13, 24, 81-8
  consequences of 134-6
  demand for 132-4
  difficulties of 134-6
  meaning of 11, 70, 138
  movement from 164-5
  part-time 24, 48, 67, 125, 133-4, 136, 161, 164, 168
  preference for 64-5
  pressures 99
  Protestant ethic 146
  provision of 165-70
  reasons for 129-32
  satisfaction 69-70, 99
  voluntary 14, 46ff, 123ff, 137, 145, 150
Wright, H. B. 22

Yoshioka, S. 101, 131, 145

Zborowski, M. 27, 54

203